The Coaching Manual

The definitive guide to the process, principles and skills of personal coaching

Julie Starr

Prentice Hall
BUSINESS

an imprint of **Pearson Education**

London • New York • Toronto • Sydney • Tokyo • Singapore • Hong Kong • Cape Town
New Delhi • Madrid • Paris • Amsterdam • Munich • Milan • Stockholm

PEARSON EDUCATION LIMITED

Edinburgh Gate
Harlow CM20 2JE
Tel: +44 (0)1279 623623
Fax: +44 (0)1279 431059
Website: www.pearsoned.co.uk

First published in Great Britain in 2003

ISBN-10: 0 273 66193 0
ISBN-13: 978 0 273 66193 1

British Library Cataloguing in Publication Data
A CIP catalogue record for this book can be obtained from the British Library.

10 9 8

Designed by Claire Brodmann Book Designs, Lichfield, Staffs
Typeset by Northern Phototypesetting Co. Ltd, Bolton
Printed and bound in Great Britain by Bell & Bain Ltd, Glasgow

The Publishers' policy is to use paper manufactured from sustainable forests.

Cw
4.10.06

The
Coaching
Manual

"In a knowledge worker age, coaching is mainstreamed.
The Coaching Manual is the most current, comprehensive,
practical, best-illustrated coaching source I have ever seen.
It compellingly teaches the mindset of keeping the
responsibility on the coachee combined with a powerful,
realistic skillset."

Dr. Stephen R. Covey, author of *The 7 Habits of Highly Effective People*

Books to make you better

Books to make you better. To make you *be* better, *do* better, *feel* better. Whether you want to upgrade your personal skills or change your job, whether you want to improve your managerial style, become a more powerful communicator, or be stimulated and inspired as you work.

Prentice Hall Business is leading the field with a new breed of skills, careers and development books. Books that are a cut above the mainstream – in topic, content and delivery – with an edge and verve that will make you better, with less effort.

Books that are as sharp and smart as you are.

Prentice Hall Business.
We work harder – so you don't have to.

For more details on products, and to contact us, visit
www.business-minds.com
www.yourmomentum.com

Contents

Acknowledgements

There are many people who have contributed to the development of the ideas and thoughts in the book and I hope I've remembered to acknowledge most of them. So I would express gratitude for the work of the following people; Anthony Robbins, Stephen Covey, Richard Bandler, John Grinder, Deepak Chopra, M. Scott Peck, Landmark Education, Brian Tracey, Frank Daniels and Milton H. Erickson.

I'd also like to thank Marcia Yudkin, Richard Watts, Scott Downing, Joss Kang, Julia Whitely, Mike Fryer and Rachael Stock for their challenges, thoughts, and ideas in preparation of the text.

chapter

1

Introduction

Personal coaching of other people is a wonderfully rewarding thing to do. Coaching is about enabling people to create change through learning. It's also about people being more, doing more, achieving more and, above all, contributing more. In our constant quest for success, happiness and fulfilment, coaching provides a way by which one person can truly support the progress of another.

So whether you're reading this book because you want to begin coaching, or simply coach more effectively, I hope you'll enjoy reading it, and find that it supports you. The field of coaching needs more of us to constantly develop our own learning, and so improve general standards of coaching everywhere.

The purpose of this book

This book explains the principles and approaches of personal coaching and shows you how to apply them in any coaching situation – from business coaching for performance, to complete life coaching. For those already coaching, the manual offers new insights and fresh ideas. For the brand new coach, the manual is a practical guide to begin and support your training. For the busy manager, the manual gives techniques to use with your team.

The manual covers the principles and beliefs that underpin coaching, describes the actual coaching process stage by stage, and gives fresh perspectives on the skills you need to develop. You'll also get practical guidance on what works and what simply gets in the way of great coaching.

If you are interested in enlisting the services of a coach, either for yourself or others, you'll also gain insight into coaching practices that will support you as a client.

Counsellors, or those thinking of going into counselling, will also find relevant information and guidance. Many of our core principles and skills are the same. Principles of integrity, and a person's responsibility for their actions are common to both. Skills of listening, questioning, establishing relationships, are also key within both professions.

A manual that helps you to learn

This book provides you with a practical, enjoyable way to learn while you read. You'll find clearly marked sections together with exercises and examples that will help you develop the skills, perspectives and beliefs of a good coach. Whether you're new to coaching, or have been coaching forever – this book will help you develop further. Some exercises are easy, while some are a real challenge. I invite you to discover which ones benefit your learning the most.

The exercises and learning routines can be done in your normal, everyday circumstances – so you don't have to be coaching in order to learn coaching! Some exercises can be done alone, others in the company of colleagues or friends. Often, you can try out the new behaviours or routines without anyone knowing you're actually learning while you're with them.

There are also routines and language that you can use in coaching sessions, to help you to be really effective in those conversations. Once you've finished reading, you can use the book as an ongoing point of reference, to help you plan your coaching, brush up on your skills, and even spot problems as they occur.

What is personal coaching?

From early forms of transportation, i.e. stagecoach, or rail coach, the word 'coaching' literally means to transport someone from one place to another. One thing that all forms of coaching seem to have in common is that people are using it to help them move forward or create change.

Put simply, coaching is a conversation, or series of conversations, one person has with another.

Put simply, coaching is a conversation, or series of conversations, one person has with another. The person who is the coach intends to produce a conversation that will benefit the other person, the coachee, in a way that relates to the coachee's learning and progress. Coaching conversation might happen in many different ways, and in many different environments.

Coaching has many different forms or expressions, within many different areas of human activity. There are sports coaches, musical coaches, relationship coaches, voice coaches, writing coaches and time-management coaches, to name but a few. It appears that whatever you might be doing, there's a coach out there to help you do it!

The person who decides whether a conversation was a coaching conversation or not is normally the person who is being coached. If someone acknowledges the following to be true after a conversation they would probably accept that it was coaching:

⇒ The focus of the conversation was primarily themselves and their circumstances.

⇒ Their thinking, actions and learning benefited significantly from the conversation.

⇒ They were unlikely to have had those benefits in thinking or learning within that time frame if the conversation hadn't happened.

So when we apply these simple principles, we realize we've been coaching each other forever. For generations, whether it's over the garden wall, a cup of tea or a beer in the pub, we've talked about what happens in our lives. We share our troubles and our dreams. We listen to each other, and we advise each other. Sometimes this process really helps. Maybe we realize a solution, make a decision, or perhaps the conversation simply makes us feel better.

Testing questions · Where are you already coaching?

Of the following, which do you do regularly?

⇒ Give friends or colleagues advice.

⇒ Listen to others' problems, to help and support them.

⇒ Explain to other people how to do something better.

⇒ Train others in new knowledge or skills.

⇒ Manage the work of others.

⇒ Give other people feedback or observations of their behaviour so that they can get better at something.

⇒ Conduct job appraisals, or assessments of people's work performance.

⇒ Give others formal counselling.

⇒ Perform personal coaching on a 1:1 basis.

This book will help improve general standards of coaching wherever they occur. Whether your coaching conversations are planned or not, this book gives you support and practical guidance so that those conversations create really great results.

Where does coaching come from?

The most recognized forms of coaching come from the sporting world. Having evolved over thousands of years, the figure of a sports coach working alongside top athletes is accepted without question. There may seem to be a contradiction in having someone who can't do what you can do, as well as you can do it, help you to improve. Andre Agassi's coach can't play tennis like Agassi does, and yet he plays a vital role in improving Agassi's game. So why does Agassi get help from a lesser player?

The reason is quite simple: because coaching is proven to work. It improves the results an individual is generating. A tennis coach needs coaching skills more than they need to be a good tennis player themselves. By applying principles of observation and feedback, sports coaches can make the difference between a world-beater and an 'also-ran'.

Strangely, where someone has all the skills needed to produce a result themselves, they can't always help someone else to do it. For example, a world-class tennis player might have real difficulty in coaching someone else to the same standard. This is because the perspectives and skills of a coach are essentially different from those of a tennis player. If a tennis player wants to become a great coach, they must begin to focus on developing coaching behaviours and skills. It's not enough to be able to 'do' – you have to be able to coach.

The same principle applies in business. Coaches work alongside individuals to help improve their performance at work, regardless of whether or not they could do that work themselves. What a coach can do, is help someone see opportunities for improvement, as well as practical ways forward.

How does personal coaching happen?

A personal coach will often work within arranged coaching sessions. The coach will normally use a blend of observation, talking, listening, questioning and reflecting back to the individual they are working with. If the situation or circumstances are suitable, a coach might also use other media, such as telephone, or e-mail.

Coaching might consist of two people talking in a room about things the coachee wants to change. This is sometimes called 'off-line' coaching. It might also be one person observing another person doing something, e.g. talking to customers or colleagues, then discussing that afterwards. This can be called on-line coaching.

Other coaching conversations might easily happen outside a formal coaching session. For example, a casual discussion around a challenging situation or goal may easily produce a conversation in which the individual receives coaching.

Whether coaching happens in the workplace or outside, the two activities can easily merge into the same thing. It's often impossible to separate work from life anyway. People's lives don't package themselves into neat little bundles – job, home, money, health, etc. Our lives seem to contain themes that run through them like common-coloured thread. If you're not happy at work, that's likely to show up somewhere else. If you're not feeling healthy or full of energy, then that's likely to be mirrored elsewhere, e.g. in your relationships or social life.

The coaching relationship

The role of coach provides a kind of support distinct from any other. A coach will focus solely on an individual's situation with the kind of attention and commitment that the individual will rarely experience elsewhere.

If you imagine yourself being coached, you will perhaps appreciate why so many people engage the services of a coach. This person, your coach, will listen to you, with a curiosity to understand who you are, what you think and generally how you experience the world. Your coach will reflect back to you, with the kind of objective view that creates real clarity. During conversations, your coach will encourage you to rise to challenges, overcome obstacles and move into action.

What's most important during that conversation is you, your success, happiness and ultimate fulfilment. Having worked to establish exactly what you want to achieve from coaching, those goals and objectives become the focus for the conversation. As a consequence, the only agenda happening in the conversation is your agenda, which your coach will often guard more closely than you do. When you're ready to quit, no longer care that you wanted to get that job, lose that weight, or have that lifestyle, your coach stays committed to those goals.

What's most important during that conversation is you, your success, happiness and ultimate fulfilment.

When things don't go well, your coach supports you. When you experience success, your coach acknowledges your achievements. Your coach will also help you to pinpoint exactly what you did that worked so well, so that you can do it again. A coaching relationship is like no other, simply because of its combination of objective detachment and commitment to the goals of the individual.

Little wonder then that so many people are finding that coaching relationships can help them develop and learn in ways that enable them to have or achieve what they really want.

Learn to coach by being coached

One of the best ways to learn how to be a good coach is to be coached. You will experience what it feels like to be a coachee. You will understand what works and what doesn't, what feels right and what feels wrong. Surprisingly, that might not always be what you expect. For example, as a coach, silence can be uncomfortable, whilst for a coachee, the same silence can feel wonderful. A sense of rapid progress during a conversation can feel great for the coach, and yet turbulent for the coachee. So if you're serious about developing your coaching skills, I recommend you get some sort of coaching as part of your development. As well as helping you develop as a coach, who knows, you might just find there are other benefits for your personal goals as well!

Coaching: In business

Coaching is now big in business. Many organizations have come to realize that they can improve both the performance and motivation of their people through coaching. Increasingly, a 'coaching' style of management is preferred to the more traditional approaches of 'command and control'. Instead of managers directing people, giving detailed instructions for what to do, and when to do it, they focus more on encouraging people to think for themselves. When problems arise, those managers who coach don't automatically jump in and solve them. Instead, they challenge others to resolve situations. These managers provide support, feedback and guidance – but rarely answers.

Managers who coach often place as much importance on the development of people reporting to them, as the tasks those people are performing. For the manager, this means fewer queues of people at their desk asking what to do next (and much less worry if the manager wants a two-week vacation). More of the manager's focus is on establishing conditions in which people can perform independently of the manager. Creating these conditions means more time is spent on activities such as objective setting, one-to-one meetings and team briefings. One-to-one meetings can now become coaching sessions, as the manager adopts a more supportive, challenging and developmental approach.

Within team meetings, the manager can use the coaching skills of listening, questioning and goal setting to encourage the group to take responsibility for situations. Over time, colleagues learn more, perform better, and are generally more motivated by this nurturing style of leadership. As they become used to the manager's expectations of them, they begin to automatically respond to situations with more responsibility and empowerment.

Managers who coach improve productivity, morale and job satisfaction for their colleagues. Such managers, in turn, find that people are less dependent upon them, which often reduces pressure, or frees up time to concentrate on other priorities. As more businesses go multi-site or even global, the distance between managers and their teams widens. Here, a coaching style is essential for both sanity and success. As a coaching manager increases people's independence, they directly reduce the dependency on themselves to be on-site, supervising what's happening.

Executive coaching

Organizations are now willing to invest in personal coaching for their senior managers and executives. By improving the performance of the most influential people within the organization, we are able to improve results at an organizational level. In short, we create a positive influence on people who have influence. Senior managers encourage typical behaviours and ways of being within the rest of their organization. What they say and how they behave establishes similar standards for people who work for them.

Executive coaching is often done by coaches operating from outside the organization, whose services are requested for an agreed duration or number of coaching sessions. Increasingly, personal coaches are also being trained internally, as organizations realize the opportunity this presents. Internal coaches normally cost less, and can operate very effectively because of their knowledge of the operation.

Within business, situations that benefit from personal coaching might include the following:

➡ A manager with potential has been promoted and is having difficulty performing in the new role.

➡ An individual is being groomed for senior management and needs to gain skills or experience before they are able to make that move.

➡ An individual has relationship issues that are creating problems at an organizational level.

➡ An organization has decided to align management behaviours to a set of core values, e.g. integrity, collaboration or innovation. Some managers will need coaching in these specific areas.

For example, during coaching a marketing director realizes he acts competitively against the sales director. Because of the competition he feels, he encourages his own department to withhold support and information from the sales department. This causes him problems. Last year he mistimed the launch of a range of sports gear – bringing it out on exactly the same day as their main competitors. Sales could have told him this was a mistake, but they heard about the launch too late. During coaching, the marketing director improves his relationship with the sales director, and encourages his department to adopt a more collaborative style.

This results in marketing telling sales more about their plans for the year, and what kind of products they're thinking of launching. As the flow and exchange of information improves, so does the quality of products and sales campaigns.

Personal coaching: Life/lifestyle

Coaching outside the workplace is now becoming common. This type of personal coaching is increasingly viewed as an acceptable form of support to anyone seeking to improve specific areas of their life, or simply their quality of life in general. Personal fulfilment, health, fitness, relationships, financial freedom are all common subjects for this type of coaching.

Why do people choose life coaching?

Coaching makes a valuable contribution to the process of helping people to experience life the way they want to experience it. For some people coaching can literally change their lives for the better. With the support of a coach, people can make clearer judgements about situations, learn more from experiences, make better choices and implement more effective decisions or actions.

For some people coaching can literally change their lives for the better.

For most of us, life can be difficult. We place tremendous pressure on ourselves to have a lot, do a lot, and be generally successful in those areas of life we consider important. That might be having a great job, having a great relationship, financial freedom – generally living a fabulous life.

I'm not going to debate whether that's right or wrong, but I do believe that coaching is a valuable counterbalance to that pressure. By enlisting the services of a coach, we can often begin to focus on what really is important to us, and begin to shape what we need to do to be more in line with that.

A comparison of coaching and therapy

There are obvious similarities between coaches and therapists. Both work with people, both do a lot of talking and listening, both deal with people's problems. However, whilst coaching and therapy work within similar areas, they are not the same thing. Coaching supports general life situations, improving our performance and creating desirable results. Therapy normally focuses on specific, significant problems, e.g. trauma, mental illness etc.

For example, coaching would be appropriate in the following situations:

➡ Putting together a life plan, understanding our aims and goals.

➡ Finding ways to reduce stress in our lives.

➡ Building a life/work balance that fulfils us.

➡ Improving our ability to relate to others.

➡ Improving our awareness of ourselves.

➡ Improving our self-discipline and motivation.

➡ Improving our health and well-being routines, e.g. diet, exercise.

There are obviously many more. What you'll notice from the above is that they are all goal-based objectives. That is, we want something we don't currently have and might use a coach to support us in attaining that. In addition, the problems associated with the goal might be making us unhappy, or even sick. For example, you're working 12-hour days on top of a 2-hour train journey and your relationship is in serious trouble because of that. In such situations, coaching is now an option where, before, therapy might have seemed to provide the only available support. Indeed, I would be surprised if a therapist would welcome clients who simply want to create more structure around their job in order to shorten their working day!

When coaching isn't the answer

It is important that a coach recognizes inappropriate situations for coaching. Where someone has issues that would be better addressed by a therapist, the coach should understand their own limitations. The skills and experience of the coach must be taken into account. As a guide, a coach with no relevant, specialist skills should avoid the following situations:

➡ Ongoing dependency on class 'A' drugs, e.g. heroin, crack, cocaine.

➡ Significant drink problems, e.g. someone drinks to get through the day.

➡ Where someone has experienced violent or sexual abuse and needs further support to deal with that.

➡ Where someone is abusing others, either physically or sexually.

➡ Mental illness, e.g. extreme and violent mood swings, ongoing depression, etc.

The skills of a therapist are often specialized to their area of therapy, e.g. addiction, abuse, mental illness, etc. To support individuals with extreme conditions or situations, a therapist will undergo specific training and development. They will normally have a relevant model, processes and terminology to deal with that situation. For example, Alcoholics Anonymous has a famous 12-step process that assists people to give up drinking. Some psychiatrists study Freudian theory, etc.

You will also notice that there is more emphasis on the 'problem' within the above situations. Often, the focus of coaching is more on 'solutions'; e.g. 'What do you want instead?' The focus during therapy tends to be more about the original, underlying problem, e.g. 'What causes you to avoid relationships?' A therapist may decide that an in-depth assessment, analysis and diagnosis of someone's problem is appropriate before the individual can progress. Whilst a level of self-awareness is also valuable within coaching, coaching doesn't rely upon an in-depth level of self-awareness in order to create results.

In summary, if a coach doesn't feel equipped to cope, they should refer the individual to a relevant specialist. If a coach does want to work in one of the above areas, then I would encourage them to go and get the relevant training and support to do that.

Chapter summary **Introduction**

Coaching has been around forever. In more recent years, we've developed it into a pro-fession. This profession focuses on techniques and methods that we understand make a difference to the results someone else is getting. Coaching is now firmly established as a way of supporting others in their quest to have what they really want, whether that is a specific goal or simply a lifestyle they want to create. Learning to coach others is both rewarding and fulfilling. And in an environment where so many of us face complex life circumstances and decisions, coaching has a valuable contribution to make.

chapter

2

Collaborative coaching

What does collaborative coaching mean?

This book is based on a collaborative style of coaching. By collaborative coaching we mean that the coach and the person being coached (referred to as the 'coachee') are working on creating changes together. As a collaborative coach, you do not 'fix' someone, solve problems for them or assume any position of superiority or higher knowledge.

The task of the coach is to use advanced skills of listening, questioning and reflection to create highly effective conversations and experiences for the individual.

Instead, the coach adopts the principle that the person being coached probably knows more about their own situation than the coach does. The coach believes in the ability of the individual to create insights and ideas needed to move their situation forward. The task of the coach is to use advanced skills of listening, questioning and reflection to create highly effective conversations and experiences for the individual.

For the person being coached, the relationship feels more like a partnership of equals, than anything parental or advisory.

Non-directive versus directive language

A collaborative coach's language is likely to be non-directive, as opposed to directive, as the following list illustrates:

Directive language	Non-directive language
'Tell me exactly what you did.'	'It might help if you speak a little more about that.'
'No – the answer you're looking for is six.'	'Perhaps tell me how you worked your answer out.'
'You need to open up to me more.'	'I notice that you don't always seem to feel comfortable discussing some things with me, and I was wondering what caused that.'

'If you want to improve your social life, you should get out more.'	➡	'What is it about your social life that you want to improve?'
'Go and join one of those singles groups on the internet – they're really good.'	➡	'What could you do to improve your social life?'
'You're still procrastinating – you simply need to get going.'	➡	'What's stopping you from getting into action here?'

A coach with a purely directive style of language assumes authority and superior knowledge in any given situation. Instructions are relayed that the individual is expected to follow. Put simply, to the coachee this feels more like being 'told' to do something, or being 'given' a new skill.

In addition, a directive coach will maintain responsibility for coming up with most of the ideas and actions within the conversation. The coach isn't so much working *with* the coachee, as working *on* the coachee. This style might sound like:

Directive conversation

COACH: 'So you say you're procrastinating, what about?'

COACHEE: 'Well I guess you'd call it administration, I mean generally, I don't like paperwork, you know, filling forms out, sending stuff off – I've a desk full of paper, it's getting out of control.'

COACH: 'Right – and you want to get it back under control quickly don't you?'

COACHEE: 'I guess I should.'

COACH: 'Well there's a number of different ways you could do that, I'd suggest that initially, you sit down and make a list of exactly what needs to be done, and make really firm commitments about when you intend to do them.'

COACHEE: (hesitates) 'Okaay . . .'

You will notice from the dialogue that most of the talking is coming from the coach, who is clearly in control of the conversation. The ideas or solutions are also coming from the coach, and the coachee is expected to comply.

A collaborative style accepts that an individual often has their own answers, and simply needs support for their own learning process.

For example, someone who constantly procrastinates or delays tasks that are important to them usually knows enough about themselves and their typical behaviours to be able to create improvement. Collaborative coaches will simply focus the individual/coachee on the relevant areas of their situation in order to surface ideas or insights needed to create learning. This style might sound like:

Non-directive conversation

COACH: 'What kind of things are you procrastinating about?'

COACHEE: 'Well I guess you'd call it administration, I mean generally, I don't like paper-work, you know, filling forms out, sending stuff off – I've a desk full of paper, its getting out of control'

COACH: 'What kind of problems does this cause you?'

COACHEE: 'All sorts, from minor embarrassments when I have to apologize, to some quite significant stuff. I once had three credit cards in a row refused simply because I'd not sent off the payments, I was left standing in a foreign airport with no way to pay for my return flight home.'

COACH: 'How else does not dealing with this stuff affect you?'

COACHEE: 'Well now that I think about it, it makes me feel a bit of a mess. I mean, an adult who can't even send off a form when I said I would, and then have to request another because I've lost the original – I make myself look pretty stupid.'

COACH: 'Okay, we've talked a bit about consequences, let's look in a different direction – what stops you from getting this stuff done?'

COACHEE: 'Well I could say I don't have time, but I don't think that's strictly true. I think it's more to do with the fact that I just hate doing it.'

COACH: 'What is it about the paperwork that you don't like?'

COACHEE: 'It's like being controlled, like someone else is making me do homework or something, when I'd rather be doing something else.'

COACH: 'That's interesting isn't it? Is that true?'

COACHEE: 'Well no, of course not, in actual fact, the reverse is probably true. If I got this stuff cleared I'd probably feel a whole lot freer and 10 pounds lighter – I could go and do whatever I wanted with a clear conscience.'

From the dialogue, you'll hear the coachee coming to their own learning, gaining their own insights and new perspectives on the situation. Note that the coach influences the focus and attention of the coachee, without telling them what to think.

In practice, an individual will feel like they've surfaced their own answers, by exploring their own thoughts and ideas in a focused way.

Directive language – advantages

It is important to be clear that a directive style of language has its uses, and can be highly effective. An example might be the case of simple skill transfer. If I can work a food blender, and you can't, you're probably not going to respond well to me exploring your thoughts or feelings about that. You simply want to know what button on the blender does what, and in what order.

Where an individual has little or no knowledge of a desired skill, and simply needs to acquire knowledge quickly, directive language is often effective. For the individual, this looks and feels more like instruction than coaching.

Within personal coaching, adopting a more directive style may sometimes be appropriate. For example, a simple piece of direct feedback may be more powerful for an individual than lots of indirect observations. Consider an individual who constantly goes off at tangents in conversation, appearing unwilling to focus on the topic they say they want to work on.

Examples of direct response or request might include:

'I notice that you often switch subjects, Jack, and I really need you to stay focused on our original topic of how you're feeling about this.'

'Jack, what he thinks isn't so important to me – simply tell me more about what you're feeling.'

Obviously for the above responses to be fully effective, the coach must have a relationship with the individual based on trust and mutual respect. The individual is then more likely to view the above responses as helpful, rather than aggressive.

Directive language – disadvantages

Within personal coaching, directive styles have many disadvantages, namely:

➡ The coachee may feel dominated or controlled, as the coach assumes a position of 'knowing better'.

➡ The coach assumes they have the best answers for the individual, and they often don't.

➡ The focus is mostly on the thoughts of the coach – this reduces the ability of the coachee to deepen their own learning in the conversation.

➡ The coach can experience significant pressure within the conversation to know everything, and be able to fix everything.

➡ The coach's focus is shifted to 'I must find the right answer' instead of 'create understanding, insight and learning' – this can result in valuable information or clues being overlooked.

➡ The coach assumes they have 'buy-in' for the suggestions they make. When they haven't, this becomes frustrating for both parties as little progress is made.

➡ The solutions from the coach might not have perfect relevance for the coachee, who may choose to view them as meaningless advice.

➡ The coachee might actually enjoy the coach being in control, if they have a tendency to avoid responsibility generally – the coach's directive style reinforces this.

Non-directive language – advantages

By creating learning for the individual from the individual, we experience the following benefits:

➡ The coachee experiences being truly listened to and appreciates the effort the coach makes to understand them.

➡ The relationship is based on equality, encouraging openness and trust. The coach is not claiming to have all the answers and the coachee feels their contribution is worthwhile.

➡ Insights, perspectives and ideas are highly relevant to the coachee, and they relate to them with both ownership and responsibility.

➡ As most ideas and actions come from the coachee, so does the responsibility for their action and results.

➡ Solutions are developed according to the understanding of the person experiencing the situation so they are normally of much higher relevance and effectiveness.

➡ Thoughts and ideas provoke ongoing learning in the mind of the coachee. As if the conversation is a pebble being thrown into a pond, questions are the catalyst that begins a reaction.

➡ If an idea doesn't get the result the coachee wanted, the coachee still feels ownership of the idea, and so will be more willing to work to get a better result.

Non-directive language – disadvantages

➡ Adopting this style of language demands an advanced level of skill on the part of the coach. Sentence structures and questions are designed to influence – and not control (more of this topic will be covered later).

➡ Until the coachee experiences the benefits of this style of conversation for themselves, they may initially become frustrated with not having the coach direct the conversation, or give them answers.

➡ The coach has much less control over what occurs during the conversation, and this can sometimes cause discomfort for both parties.

➡ The coach must be able to distinguish blatant digressions from valid topics of conversation. For example, when discussing your health, it's probably relevant for you to talk more about your food than the restaurants you go to – but not always.

➡ Conversations sometimes take longer, as the coach explores the thoughts and experiences of the coachee at the speed that the coachee is comfortable with.

Attributes of a good coach

Whether you want to develop your coaching skills further, or are thinking of using the services of a coach, you need to know how to spot those who are good, and those who are not so good. Table 2.1 begins to give us an idea of what we're looking for.

Table 2.1: Attributes of a great vs not so great coach

Great coach	Not so great coach
Is open/honest, e.g. 'Look, I think this isn't working, is it – can we look at why?'	May withhold thoughts or information, e.g. thinks: 'I think that's a crazy idea but I don't want to appear unsupportive.'
Makes someone feel listened to, valued and understood. Coachees feel buoyant, positive and optimistic following sessions.	Makes someone feel weird or strange, e.g. 'Hmm, you're a bit of an unusual case, really, aren't you?'

Helps someone tap into their own inspiration, by questioning, listening, or simply using silence.	Works hard to find the answers or solutions to the coachee's situation themselves, leaving the coachee feeling 'redundant' or 'stifled'.
Makes the coaching conversation seem effortless, i.e. maintains the conversation using appropriate responses to the coachee.	Labours to keep the conversation going or talks too much, or simply 'tries too hard'.
Focuses instinctively on the key parts of a conversation, e.g. 'Can we just stop and go back a little?'	Misses or disregards key information, perhaps wanting to 'press on' with the intention of getting a 'result'.
Remains impartial and objective throughout, e.g. 'I can see why you might think that, and I'm also interested to look at other causes of your friend's behaviour.'	Introduces judgement or prejudice into the coaching conversation, e.g. 'I agree, she obviously wanted to teach you a lesson – you're right to be angry.'
Gently probes into a situation effectively, gaining all the relevant facts, e.g. 'What specifically is it about the winter that you don't enjoy?'	Assumes they understand what the coachee means, perhaps to 'keep the conversation moving', e.g. 'Yes, I hate winter, it's just so cold isn't it?'
Builds a sense of 'relatedness' or rapport with the coachee, in order to create openness and trust.	Causes the coachee to remain guarded, or tense throughout the conversation, e.g. feeling that they have nothing in common.
Supports someone to achieve more than they would normally, i.e. without focused coaching support.	Makes little difference to the ongoing performance or results of an individual.

Is able to clarify the thoughts and goals of the coachee, e.g. 'What specifically does "more money" mean, and what is it about that that you really want?'	Leaves key thoughts or objectives vague or unclear in the mind of the coachee, e.g. 'Okay, so you want more money, let's look at how we're going to get you that.'
Is encouraging and challenging, whilst realistic about situations, e.g. 'Two weeks to make all the calls would be great, I'm just wondering what would happen if you got that done in a week instead – what would that feel like?'	Creates either a lack of encouragement and challenge, or undue pressure, e.g. 'Aww, come on, how long does it take to make a few calls? – you could have those done by tomorrow if you actually tried.'
Holds someone to account, in order to create a constant focus on the coachee's objectives, e.g. 'Okay, again you said by the time we next met, you'd have had the salary conversation with your manager – let's look at what's stopping you from having it.'	Allows themselves to be 'fobbed off' or sidetracked from issues of broken commitment, perhaps in order to maintain rapport. For example, 'Well, that's ok, you're really busy, can you do it when things calm down a bit?'
Is happier to achieve lasting results over time, than fast results that don't last.	Feels like they've failed if they don't see immediate results from the coaching.
Uses words and phrases that influence the individual positively, e.g. 'So imagine yourself speaking to an audience and this time you really enjoyed it – what would that feel like?	Uses words clumsily and causes the coachee to feel negative or uncomfortable, e.g. 'Yes, your lack of confidence does seem to be a problem.'

Places real importance on the coachee's comfort and well-being during the session, e.g. 'Look, this has been fairly intense – do you need a break, can I get you a coffee?'	Mixes considerations about the coachee with other priorities, e.g. leaves their mobile phone switched on during a session.
Leads by example, e.g. shows up on time, calls when they said they would, keeps any commitments made, or makes amends when they don't.	Displays double standards, e.g. shows up late, uses weak excuses, isn't prepared for the session, etc.

A great coach is able to make the process of coaching look almost effortless.

Now that's obviously not an exhaustive list, although it does give you an idea of how a good coach can be distinguished from one who isn't so good.

To summarize, the attributes of a good coach can be highlighted in three key areas:

➡ What a coach does – their actual behaviour.

➡ Principles or beliefs a coach operates from, maybe relating to themselves as a coach, to the coachee and also to the coaching process, e.g. 'coaching works for everyone.'

➡ What a coach is able to do – their skills and knowledge.

From the outside, a great coach is able to make the process of coaching look almost effortless, like an easy, natural conversation.

Chapter summary **Collaborative coaching**

Collaborative coaching is a wonderful coaching style because of its supportive, less directive approach. Whilst more directive styles can be really effective, they demand a coach to be much more confident about both the coaching relationship, and their own expertise and relevant knowledge. In collaborative coaching, the coachee is called upon to generate their thoughts, insights and ideas, which they often experience as incredibly liberating. For any coach, to be a less directive coach is challenging, demanding and highly skilful when done effectively. For the individual being coached, it is often a profound experience that can literally change their life.

Coaching principles or beliefs

Operating principles for coaches

From my experiences and observations of coaching, I notice that there appears to be an underlying set of guidelines and assumptions that support collaborative coaching. A room may be full of fabulous coaches who all look different, sound different and appear different. However, when they coach, they are operating from a group of assumptions and beliefs that are common. For example, they all believe in the power of coaching, and they all believe that they can coach. These assumptions and beliefs are what help define effective coaching. The coaching principles I'd like to cover in this chapter are:

coaching principles

➡ Maintain a commitment to support the individual.

➡ Build the coaching relationship on truth, openness and trust.

➡ The coachee is responsible for the results they are generating.

➡ The coachee is capable of much better results than they are currently generating.

➡ Focus on what the coachee thinks and experiences.

➡ Coachees can generate perfect solutions.

➡ The conversation is based on equality.

Once we've identified this common set of beliefs, they serve as principles we can operate from, to achieve effectiveness over time. By reflecting on them, and comparing them with our own behaviours and approach, we can often spot opportunities to improve. When sometimes coaching isn't successful, they can also help us to understand why. Take the example of a coachee who seems to be happy to spend the whole coaching session complaining about his situation at work. In addition, the coachee refuses to consider potential solutions or what they might be doing to make things better. The coach tries everything they can think of to help the coachee feel more positive about the situation, and get into action to sort things out. Then, by reflecting on the following principles, the coach is reminded to coach from the assumption that the coachee is responsible for their circumstances and actions. It may be that the coach was getting so frustrated with the whole situation that they forgot to focus on that simple principle. Sometimes issues within coaching can appear complex, when really a simple approach solves the mightiest of problems.

Some of the key principles occur as rules of behaviour a coach must remember, while others appear as perspectives of what the coach is there to do, or not do. Where a coach is consistently able to adopt these principles, this will improve their ability to coach effectively over time.

Maintain a commitment to support the individual

A good coach must want to coach the individual, and remain committed to the coaching relationship. They must maintain a supportive attitude towards the coachee, or consider withdrawing from the assignment.

At the beginning of the coaching relationship, this appears fairly easy. The coach is probably thinking more about how to make the assignment successful, than whether they do or do not want to help the coachee with their situation. As time moves on, the coach may experience several different factors that encourage them to withdraw their support. That may or may not be something the coach is aware of. For example, simple fatigue with the coaching conversations and even the coachee themselves may creep in. Where the coaching process feels laboured, and is perhaps showing little sign of progress, the coach might begin to withdraw their commitment, even without knowing it. For the coach, this may feel like a kind of resignation or boredom. It's important that coaches are almost self-coaching in this instance. They must regularly evaluate where they are in their coaching relationships, and identify any negative thoughts or beliefs about these relationships.

If that sounds like analyzing analysis, it needn't be. When I'm coaching, I like to have a couple of minutes' preparation before the coachee arrives. In that time, I'll read through my notes from previous sessions, reflecting on what the individual's goals are, and remind myself how I'm contributing to that. It gets me into the mental mode of supporting the individual, regardless of how challenging the session might be.

Coaching from non-judgement

On a tougher note, the coach may decide that they do not actually like the person they are coaching very much! Remember, as humans, we have a natural tendency to judge others. We compare how someone else looks, thinks or acts, with how we do. We might approve or disapprove of other people because of their hair, clothes, appearance, the words they use, their tone of voice, etc.

What if a coach disapproves of the person they are coaching? What if they hear of behaviour that they think is bad or wrong? A coach might hear of lying, cruelty, and infidelity – any of which might encourage them to judge the individual as 'wrong' in some way.

Let's not debate whether any of those behaviours are 'wrong' or 'right'. As a coach, any disapproval impairs the ability to facilitate the process of a coaching conversation. In addition, the coach's disapproval usually communicates itself to the coachee – even if they don't voice it directly.

For example, imagine that a coach is working with an individual who reminds them very strongly of a domineering ex-partner. This coachee says something like 'You see, I have certain standards I will always live by' and the coach remembers that's exactly what their ex-partner used to say! Before long, the coach is comparing them to their ex-partner, and beginning to dislike them intensely.

The coach begins to have internal thoughts or dialogue about what the coachee is saying, e.g. 'Ooh – that's just what they used to do' or, 'you must be difficult to live with'. This internal dialogue blocks your ability to listen fully, like trying to watch TV with the radio on.

Where we do not see someone objectively, with an open mind, we are less likely to begin to understand them. This lack of understanding has a direct impact on our ability to relate to the individual, and how things are for them. At the same time, we've diminished rapport, and so reduced our ability to influence the other person.

The other person is likely to sense the coach's disapproval of them, possibly from facial expression, tonality, gestures or simply the phrases the coach is using, e.g. 'So why did you do that?' As the coachee recognizes disapproval, they become more guarded in their responses.

Once a coach starts to see the coachee as 'flawed' in some way, they begin to adopt the role of 'fixer'. Again, the coachee is likely to sense this, and perhaps feel defensive or uncomfortable.

Where a coach's ability to relate to and understand someone is key to their success, judgement becomes a real stumbling block. Instead the coach must work at simply observing the coachee objectively – without judgement. When a coach maintains a more neutral, open posture, they can gather much clearer information and so gain more relevant insights into the situation. A coach's own thoughts will be clearer, and they may even feel calmer, as they gradually begin to appreciate how it is for the person they're coaching. They aren't thinking things they can't voice, and generally their mind remains quieter during the conversation.

A coach's role is not to judge or disapprove of the way your coachee treats other people, or indeed how they live their life.

A coach's role is not to judge or disapprove of the way your coachee treats other people, or indeed how they live their life. A coach's role is simply to make clear links between the behaviours the individual is generating, and the results they are getting. For example, the coachee might have aspirations of promotion at work, and knows the reason this isn't happening is strongly linked to the lack of support he is getting from his peer group. He discusses several confrontations with these colleagues, and describes cruel things he's said, to 'get back at' or hurt people.

It's a very simple link for the coach to make between the person's goals and his current behaviour. However, if the coach spends energy on convincing the coachee that his behaviour towards others is 'wrong' in some way, the individual may easily reject the suggestion. Far more straightforward and motivating for the individual is to highlight the fact that his behaviour simply doesn't work and has a direct impact on his goals. We then have the opportunity to discuss more positive behaviours that will benefit him, and his colleagues.

What does non-judgement feel like for a coach?

Well, put simply, to be in non-judgement feels like nothing, because there's nothing going on! The coach is not having internal dialogue along the lines of 'that's awful, cruel, dumb etc.'. The coach is not frowning with disapproval, shaking their head or making little 'tutting' noises. Instead, they are really listening and staying with the flow of the conversation.

Hopefully, judgement is replaced by a pervading sense of curiosity, towards what is being said and what the individual is experiencing. The coach's overriding sense of purpose is to seek to understand what's really happening, and what's relevant or important about that, given the goals of the coachee.

How do we let go of judgement?

Unless you've spent years gaining the enlightenment of a Buddhist master, I think you're going to have to accept a lifelong journey with this one. You will judge others, but the trick is to notice that you're doing that, and give it up whenever you catch yourself doing so.

The following exercise will help you practise.

Coach's toolkit	Meditation for non-judgement
What is this?	➡ A way of practising letting go of judgements we make about others and allowing our minds to clear.
When would I use it?	➡ Whenever you can observe someone else. For example: – Someone making a speech or presentation. – Someone who's talking to someone else. – Someone involved in a group discussion, e.g. a business meeting.
Why would I do this?	– To develop a more objective view of someone else's situation. – To help you relate to someone else more closely, e.g. when coaching someone else. – To create a stiller, clearer mind when listening.

Stage one – become aware

1   Find someone who's appropriate for you to observe. You should be in the same room or setting as they are, and be able to see and hear them clearly. Ideally, you should be able to observe them without being interrupted, e.g. by having to speak or join a discussion. Have a notepad and pen ready in case you feel like taking notes.

2   Remain relaxed and focused. Let your breathing be steady, and your posture relaxed yet upright. Begin to watch or take notice of the other person.

3   As you watch the person you're studying, begin to notice your own thoughts. What are you thinking or saying to yourself? Just notice, that's all, e.g:

➡ I agree/ disagree?

➡ I like/don't like?

➡ I've heard this before.

➡ He/she reminds me of . . . .

Notice your own thoughts with detachment, almost as if they weren't yours, as though you are observing yourself observing.

Stage two – let go of your own thoughts

4   As you notice your thoughts, let them go. Acknowledge a thought, then let it pass. Like something floating past you on a stream, allow it to be there, then let it go again. If it helps, write down any thoughts as you notice them and then allow them to pass.

Stage three – use intention to guide your attention

5   Use one or two of the following to guide and refocus your thoughts:

➡ What is this person saying?

➡ How does this person feel about this?

➡ What is this person committed to?

Toolkit Summary   **Mediation for non-judgement**

This exercise isn't easy! – However the potential benefits are worth the effort. If you're finding it difficult to do steps one to three all in one go, perhaps just do the first one for a while. When that becomes easier, add the second step. Finally, when you've mastered steps one and two, then add step three.

The key is to develop an awareness and detachment of our own thoughts and judgements. It's called a meditation because it follows the simple principles of basic meditations, i.e. observing our own thoughts and allowing them to pass. Another way of developing this detachment would be to simply practise meditation.

Once we allow ourselves to detach from our own thoughts or judgements about another person, we can stop those thoughts getting in the way of something else we want to do, e.g. listening to the client.

coaching principles

Build the coaching relationship on truth, openness and trust

When you step into a coaching relationship, you seek to honestly serve the individual you are coaching. This is worth mentioning, as our integrity in this issue can be so easily corrupted.

One easy trap to fall into can occur when the person requesting and paying for your services isn't the person getting the coaching. This often happens in business, where a more senior individual has requested coaching for a colleague. I'll tell you about Clive as an example.

Coach's story

Clive's manager, Mark, asked me to give Clive a series of coaching sessions. Mark felt that Clive needed to deliver faster results, and develop better relationships at work.

So here I have a set of coaching objectives already established for someone who may, or may not, want coaching. From the outset it was important to let Clive, the coachee, know exactly what had been his manager's thinking that led to my involvement. Working with his manager, we discussed the specific areas of improvement that were to be the focus of the coaching activity, and what would be involved during coaching. We established that the coaching was a form of support that Clive could either accept, or refuse, at any point during the process.

In addition, we spent time looking at the coaching as an opportunity that Clive could benefit from, and added his own objectives into the coaching. I explained what kind of updates I'd be giving his manager, and assured him that the specific content of conversations would be disclosed to no one.

With Mark, the person paying my bill, I agreed that whilst I was happy to discuss general areas of discussion and progress, I would disclose nothing of the actual content of my conversations with Clive. We also agreed that if Mark wanted any more information, he'd ask Clive directly.

During coaching conversations, Clive welcomed the chance to discuss his situation. In short, Clive wasn't even sure if he wanted to stay with the organization, and especially doubted his ability to build teams.

My focus during those conversations had to be to first establish what was best for Clive, and then work out how that related to his manager and the company he was currently working for. We worked through several different possibilities, including scenarios where he imagined leaving or applying for other positions.

If that sounds disloyal to my client (Mark), let me stress that this is the only principle we can effectively coach someone from. Had I tried to influence Clive to stay, or to take on more of the responsibilities that his manager wanted him to, I would have immediately corrupted the relationship between him and myself.

There was also the question of maintaining integrity between the sponsor, Mark, and myself. From the outset, I made it clear how coaching works, and the ground rules of the coaching activity. Most sponsors accept that they won't be party to the content of conversations. A coach must simply agree with a sponsor on how they'll be updated and then let the coachee know that will be happening.

One option for sharing the content of coaching discussions is for the coach to encourage regular conversations between the sponsor and the coachee. This often builds openness and so trust between them, which benefits their working relationship.

As a simple rule, never say anything about your coachee or client that you would not want them to hear about afterwards.

> **As a simple rule, never say anything about your coachee or client that you would not want them to hear about afterwards.**

In case you're wondering about what happened to Clive, well, he decided to stay and make more of the opportunities that were right in front of him. Time spent on balancing the different options and potential pitfalls or benefits enabled him to reach this decision.

By helping him to appreciate that he always had options, he was able to let go of the 'trapped' feelings he had due to the 'pressures' placed upon him by his manager. Through the process of discussion, Clive could hear that Mark's expectations for him sounded more like encouragement than pressure.

Testing questions | Rating openness and honesty

Ask yourself these questions to help you understand levels of openness and honesty in a relationship (this is especially useful if you can use an existing coaching relationship):

Q Did you ever say anything to the other person that wasn't true (aka a lie)?

Q Do you ever avoid talking about any subject or situation with the other person?

Q Do you feel the other person ever avoids talking about certain things with you?

Q Have you ever said anything about the other person that you wouldn't want them to hear?

Q How freely expressive are you able to be when you're with the other person?

Q How comfortable are you in this person's company?

coaching principles

The coachee is responsible for the results they are generating

We coach from the principle that an individual is ultimately responsible for their lives and the results they're getting. That includes their job, the relationship they've chosen, where they're living, etc. If we acknowledge we are responsible for something, it follows that we have power and influence over it. For example, if I acknowledge that I am responsible for how good a job I have, then it's up to me to do something about it if I'm not happy.

An individual is ultimately responsible for their lives and the results they're getting.

As a coaching principle, this sense of personal responsibility is key if we are to empower individuals to act powerfully and positively in their own situations. It is useful to break the word itself into two halves, as it literally becomes 'response' and 'ability' – in other words, the ability to respond.

Victim postures

The opposite of this responsible, powerful posture is victim posture. People who adopt a victim-like posture act as though life were something that happens 'to' them, and they can do little or nothing to influence it. In their language and behaviours it might show up as statements like 'Well, what can I do about it?' or 'This seems to keep happening to me', or 'It's pointless, there's not much I can do about it anyway.'

As a consequence of their diminished sense of responsibility, people with a victim-like posture in a situation may also tend to blame others. For example, 'My partner stops me from leading my life as I really want to' or 'My life hasn't worked out because of my childhood' or 'It's not fair.'

From a coaching perspective, a victim-like posture will impair the coachee's ability to imagine that they have real influence over how their lives are going, and the results they are experiencing. Coachees acting as a victim will perceive far fewer possibilities for themselves in a difficult situation. They may see no way out of situations and no point in attempting to find one.

Where many of the issues you will be discussing during a coaching conversation are potentially emotive, the assumption that we are responsible for how our lives are going is not easy for many people to accept. For example, where someone comes from a violent background, has money problems and has just been fired, it's difficult to encourage them to take a responsible view of their current situation.

As a coach, it's important to remember that it's a principle we're using, and not necessarily the truth. To readily blame others for how our lives have turned out doesn't tend to make us feel very powerful. Instead, we feel like victims at the mercy of the twists and turns of life.

When we adopt a perspective of responsibility for our situations, we immediately feel like we have some power and influence over them. In the example of redundancy, this type of situation often forms a crossroads for people. Some people prosper from the situation, choosing positive action or responses, which cause the apparent cloud to have a silver lining. Such responses might include changing careers, going out and finding a better job, returning to education etc.

Other people aren't quite as resourceful in their response to redundancy, spending time blaming others, or arguing that there's not much they can actually do. A person who adopts a responsible approach to the situation is immediately more powerful than one with a victim-like stance.

Responsibility is not blame

It is important to be clear that responsibility is not the same as blame. Blame implies that someone has done something wrong, and should possibly suffer as a result. Blame is also associated with shame, guilt and suffering. Responsibility, however, is simply about acknowledging our own influence in situations, and as a coach you must create a clear distinction between the two.

If a coachee takes on blame instead of responsibility, this does little to create a sense of personal power. More often, they are likely to feel worse about something, e.g. worthless or bad. Where someone has a tendency to adopt a martyr-like posture to situations, this really doesn't help.

A martyr-like posture would tend towards feeling 'bad' or 'burdened'. For example, 'Oh that's typical of me – I'm just useless', or 'I always end up doing something like this, I suppose that's just my lot in life, and I just have to put up with it.'

Watch for the victim and martyr language in the following example:

COACH: 'Perhaps tell me a little more about what happened in your relationship.'

COACHEE: 'Well, basically, they dumped me with no warning. Things seemed absolutely fine when "Wham!" I get a note on the kitchen table, no sorry, no nothing.'

COACH: 'I guess you must have felt pretty bad at that point.'

COACHEE: 'Tell me about it – I feel terrible! I'm not sleeping, not eating – what am I supposed to do now?'

COACH: 'What do you think went wrong?'

COACHEE: 'Who knows? It seemed like one minute I was living with someone and the next minute they've upped and gone. I wouldn't care, this is the third time this has happened to me, life seems to be dealing me a pretty bad hand right now.'

You will notice from the dialogue that the coachee feels that this is simply something that's happened to them and that they are the victim in the scenario.

As coach, it may sometimes be appropriate to ask your coachee to adopt a more powerful posture, by 'trying on' this principle of responsibility with you, i.e. acting as if it were true. Then examine a situation from this perspective, to discover new insights or learning:

COACH: 'If you were to adopt a perspective of responsibility for what happened in the relationship, what would you see?'

COACHEE: 'I'm not sure what you mean – why would I do that?'

COACH: 'Well, it might help a little with getting more information that we can use.'

COACHEE: 'Okay, well, my partner was always saying that I wasn't really committed to things working out, that I didn't put enough into it.'

COACH: 'OK – what else?'

COACHEE: 'Well, my partner thought we should talk more, about how things were going, if there was anything we weren't happy about – you know the kind of stuff.'

COACH: 'What was your response to that?'

COACHEE: 'Well, at the time I said it was rubbish, why would anyone want to do that?'

COACH: 'Is there anything you'd add to that now?'

COACHEE: 'Huh – yeah, I guess I should have stayed more aware of where my partner was at, at least that way I'd have known we'd got problems.'

Now this might not be enough to save a relationship, but it may well create learning of a better quality than could be achieved by simply staying with a victim's perspective. From the dialogue above, you'll notice that the coachee sounds more powerful, more in control later in the dialogue. He/she is discussing things within their own influence, namely whether they committed to the relationship or didn't, whether they talked to their partner or not.

Ultimately, when we're working with an individual to create change in their lives, this kind of fresh perspective may be just what's needed to cast new light onto a situation.

Testing questions **Responsible or victim?**

If you want to coach someone from a principle of responsibility, then I recommend you be able to relate to that principle personally first. These questions can help you understand your own ability to take responsibility for yourself and your situations. Simply think about them for a while, then consider each question in turn:

Q Do you frequently blame other people or things for your problems?

Q Are you able to make links to your own behaviours and the results you get? E.g. I didn't put a ticket on my car so I got fined.

Q Do you prefer complaining about problems rather than talking about solutions?

Q In conversation, do you 'own' your own problems? E.g. 'I need to do something about this.'

Q Do you complain that things 'aren't fair' or can you view situations more objectively?

If this is difficult for you to think about, maybe ask someone whom you trust for their opinion. Or next time you're discussing a problem or situation you want to change, notice how much you talk about that as a responsible, powerful person – or how much you simply moan and complain!

The coachee is capable of much better results than they are currently generating

A coach must believe that the individual they are working with is capable of being more, doing more and having more, especially in relationship to their stated goals. That might be anything from increased fitness, to a lasting relationship, a better job etc. If a coach secretly believes the coachee is unlikely to succeed in their objectives, feeling that they're simply not capable – then that simple belief is likely to undermine the coaching process.

For example, imagine as a coach you're working with someone who says they want to be able to speak confidently and powerfully to groups. After some initial discussions, you agree to work with them to achieve this goal.

As the coaching progresses, you hear them make some attempts at a speech, and decide that the person is really awful, very nervous and you can't imagine the possibility of their ever giving a successful talk in public.

At this point, your ability to support the individual to achieve their goal becomes inherently flawed. You have a negative expectation of the outcome of the coaching, and this is probably going to get in the way during conversations. You might already know that when parents or teachers have a positive expectation of children, the children achieve better results than where the reverse is true.

Whilst it isn't an identical situation, I strongly believe that the same principle easily affects coaching, either of children or adults. As coach, if you say one thing, and think another, somehow that communicates. Maybe through expression, tonality or gestures, your coachee will sense that you don't actually believe that they're capable of achieving their goals.

As coach, if you say one thing, and think another, somehow that communicates.

In a worst case scenario, you may even undermine their confidence, and make the achievement of their goals less likely. This must constitute the reverse of coaching!

Now, in some cases it may be quite appropriate for a coach to form this view. Coachees may set goals that you genuinely feel are unrealistic, or place too much pressure upon them. Be careful, however, not to place your *own* limitations upon other people.

For example, imagine you're coaching someone who tells you they want to double their income within the next six months. Now whilst this kind of income increase rarely happens, it is actually very possible. It's up to you to decide whether you're willing to enter into a coaching agreement to support them to achieve this. To do so, you must believe that they are capable of creating the increase.

Do you say yes to the work, secretly believing the coachee isn't capable? Do you tell them you think it's not possible, but you're willing to coach them into a more likely goal, and risk losing the work? This begins to surface the question of integrity, doesn't it? (By integrity, I simply mean being of your word, i.e. telling your truth and doing what you say you'll do.)

I would suggest that where you're sure that something isn't possible for the person you're coaching you deal with it honestly. If you allow yourself to enter into a coaching relationship where you haven't told the truth about how you feel, then the integrity of the relationship is corrupted.

As a coach, you would be constantly having second thoughts about what you had committed to, and whether or not things were going to 'work out'. Again, this is going to affect your ability to challenge and encourage the coachee in an honest manner.

For the coachee, having a coach who secretly feels that the coachee is going to fail is not the kind of support needed!

coaching principles

Testing questions | **Are you a support or saboteur?**

Think about an existing relationship where you coach or support the goals of someone else. The following questions will help you consider your levels of commitment to this person:

Q How do you feel about the goals this person has described?

Q How achievable do you believe this person's goals are?

Q Do you believe this person will really benefit from the results they want to produce?

Q How do you feel about the person you're coaching?

Focus on what the coachee thinks and experiences

The focus of coaching conversations should be on the coachee and not the coach. Does that sound obvious? It is possible for coaching conversations to be all about what the coach thinks, knows, does, as though the coach were an example to be followed.

When someone calls themselves 'a coach', that can set an expectation of what being a coach should mean. Maybe people imagine that a coach has sage-like wisdom, or limitless knowledge (that's not true by the way!). For example, a coachee may think a coach has seen their sort of situation before, and so knows what to do. They may imagine that the coach knows more about life, how to be happy, how to be successful or fulfilled.

Added to that, if as a coach you have experienced getting some great results with a few coaching conversations, it can be quite easy for success to go to your head.

Perhaps a coachee might ask a coach, 'What would **you** do in this situation?' This is an unintentional trap, laid to catch the coach's ego. The coach's ego hears this and purrs – imagining that someone actually wants to know what they think, so that they can be more like them.

Remember that a collaborative coach is not there to tell people what they should do, or have them make choices based on their life and preferences. In collaborative coaching, you're working with someone, to help them get where they want to go.

The principal focus has to remain on the coachee's thoughts and objectives, as those are the reason the conversation is taking place. If, when coaching, I hear myself 'taking over' the conversation, introducing my beliefs and views or giving 'advice', I begin to feel uncomfortable, as I know I'm shifting the emphasis of the conversation.

As with all principles, occasionally I'll find reasons to work outside it. An example might be where the individual appears reluctant to share their experiences. Offering my own experiences or thoughts can create a greater sense of sharing and trust.

An exercise **But enough of me – let's talk about you!**

Next time you're having a casual conversation with someone, begin to notice the change in focus of the discussion from them to you. In other words, are you talking about your experiences and thoughts, or theirs? If it's appropriate, keep the focus of the conversation completely on them for a while, e.g. what they've been doing, what they've been experiencing, what their thoughts and opinions are etc. After the conversation, ask yourself:

Q How comfortable am I when I'm not contributing my own thoughts and ideas?

Q How much did I have to resist adding what I thought or knew into the conversation?

Q What effect did it have when I concentrated only on what they said or thought?

Coachees can generate perfect solutions

As humans we have an almost childlike wish to be the person who comes up with the best thought, the cleverest answer or the winning idea. Like at school, where praise and reward come to those with the 'right' answer.

In collaborative coaching, the rules of your game are subtly different. To continue the classroom metaphor, you apply all your learning and experiences to make sure that the person next to you comes up with the answer. That may or may not be the answer that you'd thought of. Clear ownership of the answer rests with the other person, who will normally go and use it on their own, to get what they want, together with the praise and reward.

As a coach, you win when someone else does. Your pleasure comes from being part of someone else's process, and helping them see different ways in which they can create the results they want. This becomes incredibly fulfilling for the coach, and a huge motivation to continue coaching.

In practical terms, solutions or ideas spoken by the person being coached are often more reasonable, pragmatic and likely to be formed into action. That person will usually feel greater ownership of the idea, and link that to a sense of responsibility for its success.

For example, I might be coaching a working mother having problems juggling her life between work and home. We may have explored lots of different aspects of the situation, in order to understand the different values and factors involved.

As an observer, I might have the idea of changing her childcare centre, as this seems to be causing the problems. I might advise this, with the following potential consequences:

➡ It's a perfect idea for the coachee, and she seizes it immediately.

➡ She rejects the idea because she has a 'polarity response' to advice, i.e. automatically takes an opposing view.

➡ She rejects the idea because it doesn't feel right to her, or make practical sense to her.

➡ She initially accepts the idea then disregards it later.

➡ She accepts the idea, switches to another care centre, but that makes things much worse and she then blames me.

➡ She accepts the idea, and disregards her own instinct, which was to involve her mother in the situation.

A coach can resist the temptation to always have the answers. A good coach will often operate from the perspective that the best quality solutions come from the coachee, not the coach. The coach will still influence those ideas and insights. The process of a coach's involvement guarantees this. The coach's most common tools of influence are still questioning, listening, observation and reflection.

The coach's most common tools of influence are still questioning, listening, observation and reflection.

When we work with the rule consistently, however, we also develop an understanding of when to break it. I would recommend that a coach stay mostly out of advice, and not 'tell' people what they 'should' do. Infrequently I'll ask permission to offer a suggestion, e.g. 'Can I offer a thought?' then 'How would switching your childcare centre affect the situation?'

By requesting permission, you're increasing the probability that the other person will accept your idea, whilst acknowledging the intrusion.

Once you've offered the suggestion, let it go. Don't become attached to their agreeing to it. They may or may not go with your idea, and that might be immediately, or some time afterwards.

Above all, remember to give up the idea of 'appearing smart' by having the 'right' answer. In the above situation, the best solution for the coachee may well have been their own idea to involve their mother, because of factors the coach wasn't aware of. The person's mother might welcome the opportunity to spend more time with their grand-children, be flexible when and where they looked after the children, and do all this for free. Until now, the coachee's mother may not have offered her services as she respected her daughter's need for independence.

A collaborative coach needs to temper a basic human instinct to be 'right' about something. By giving up an attachment to finding a solution to a coachee's problem, we are actively encouraging them to find their own solution. Collaborative coaching encourages someone to be more powerful, more creative and more in action around situations, by helping them to find their own ways forward.

An exercise **Help someone else find the answer**

For this exercise, you'll need to have a casual conversation with someone where they are discussing a problem or frustration. You can have this conversation by asking someone to do this, or you could wait for the next time one happens naturally. It will be a conversation where the other person is not asking you to solve their problem, they're just talking, or complaining about it. For example, maybe they're too busy, too tired all the time, fed up with their job, etc.

Rules of the game

During the conversation, you **must not** give them any advice or suggestions for a way forward. No matter how great your ideas or advice, just pretend for a while that you don't have an answer – and they do.

Step one – display the relevant facts

Ask them questions until you've (both) heard what you feel to be the 'key' or relevant facts about the situation, e.g. 'What's causing this?' 'How supportive is your boss?' 'What actually is the real problem here?' If observations work better than questions, then use them, e.g. 'You seem to be spending a long time out of the office.'

Step two – discover their answer

When you feel you've got enough information for them to answer the following questions, use whichever seems appropriate:

➡ 'What are you considering doing about this?'

➡ 'What do you need to fix this/sort it all out?'

➡ 'What could you do to improve the situation?'

➡ 'What options do you have?'

Or any other question that requires them to think of their own solution to their situation.

Step three

(This step is optional.) If you are still 100 per cent convinced that you have a better answer, the right answer, and that they will benefit tremendously from hearing it, then tell them. Perhaps use one of the following phrases to link to the previous part:

➡ 'Can I offer an idea?'

➡ 'As you were talking, I've thought of something that might help. What if . . .'

➡ 'You know, another answer might be to . . .'

Sanity warning

This can be a difficult exercise! – Especially if you're used to solving other people's problems for them. We can feel quite awkward or uncomfortable not 'fixing' things for people. So if the conversation isn't going well, e.g:

➡ The discussion isn't flowing naturally.

➡ You can't think of the right questions or observations.

➡ They really (definitely) can't think of any ways forward.

Give up, and have a go another day! Go back to having a normal, casual conversation, e.g. give your own views, experience, ideas, etc.

Alternatively, do step one on its own, then add step two when it feels right. Simply ask a few more questions than you would normally, before suggesting something. Before long, you'll find that feels more natural, as you feel less compelled to give your idea or advice. Then when that bit feels comfortable, simply ask them what their solution is, perhaps using some of the suggestions in step two.

The conversation is based on equality

coaching principles

As coach, you're working together with someone else, to give them support in achieving something that they want. Your relationship will feel more like a partnership of equals, than anything parental or advisory.

As you continue to work with someone, you strengthen the process of coaching. Together, you explore situations, causes, barriers and ways forward. The person you are coaching must feel they are receiving constant support, whilst remaining your equal. They must feel free to make requests or contribute to the discussion at all times.

Where coaches adopt the unfortunate posture of superiority, e.g. 'trust me – I know about this' or 'hey, I really think you should listen to me on this one' not only can they alienate the coachee, but they also run the risk of giving poor or irrelevant advice.

This imbalanced approach can also undermine the coachee's confidence, as they begin to feel subordinate in the relationship. Alternatively, they may dislike the inference that the coach is somehow 'superior' in matters relating to their own situation. Even where people are actually quite comfortable with a subordinate role, you diminish their ability to own their own problems, or seek their own solutions.

By acting from a sense of equality and collaboration, we promote an environment where the truth can be told, mistakes made and insights discovered.

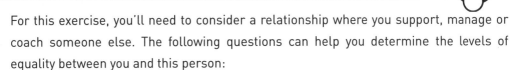

Testing questions **Are we equal?**

For this exercise, you'll need to consider a relationship where you support, manage or coach someone else. The following questions can help you determine the levels of equality between you and this person:

Q How much do you respect or admire this person?

Q If you weren't managing or coaching this person, how comfortable would you feel asking this person for advice?

Q If this person really wanted to do something, and you told them you didn't agree with that, what would they do?

➡ Go ahead and do it anyway.

➡ Ask you more about your views before making a decision.

➡ Go with your decision, as they will assume you 'know better'.

Chapter summary **Coaching principles or beliefs**

Coaches operate from principles of success, in much the same way as sportspeople or businesspeople do. To repeat the key principles:

➡ Maintain a commitment to support the individual.

➡ Build the coaching relationship on truth, openness and trust.

➡ The coachee is responsible for the results they are generating.

➡ The coachee is capable of much better results than they are currently generating.

➡ Focus on what the coachee thinks and experiences.

➡ Coachees can generate perfect solutions.

➡ The conversation is based on equality.

Coaching process and structure

Building a good supporting structure or process is key to the overall success of a coaching assignment. Several factors that alter the effectiveness of coaching are independent of what actually happens in each session. These factors include length of sessions, duration between sessions, keeping appropriate notes and records, etc.

In addition, the initial coaching sessions will be distinct from, say, the final session as the objectives for those sessions are different. At the beginning of a coaching assignment we're placing more emphasis on seeking to understand the coachee and their goals. By the final sessions we're consolidating our learning, and finding ways to continue learning. A good coach will appreciate the overall coaching cycle they are working within and be able to maintain a view of this 'bigger picture' when needed.

Understandably, coachees like to know they are receiving a quality service from a coach with professional standards they can rely on. Building a foundation for coaching that is mutually understood and agreed helps with this perception of the coach's services. No matter how skilled the coach is within coaching conversations, if the coach is managing the overall situation badly, then the coachee is going to be disappointed. For example, if the coach can't remember what was discussed in the previous session, or recall basic facts about the individual's goals, this can easily cause frustration for the coachee.

By agreeing on how the coach will operate, the coach esures that some basic standards are met. By introducing a certain amount of structure to an assignment, a coach can aim for standards such as the following:

1   *The coachee understands key information relating to the coaching*: it is important that the coachee knows as much information as they need to feel comfortable and enthusiastic about the coaching relationship they're entering into. This might include a basic knowledge of what coaching is, or simply how often sessions are going to be and how long they'll last.

2   *The coach demonstrates a commitment to the coachee's success or learning*: the coachee needs to know that the coach is working hard for them, focusing on their progress and taking their development very seriously. The coachee may view various things as signs of this commitment, e.g. the coach's enthusiasm and energy during sessions, or simply the fact that the coach turns up on time.

3   *The coach develops an approach tailored to the coachee*: the coachee needs to feel that the coach is approaching them as an individual, and adapting their approach accordingly. This would include requesting the coachee's views as to what is working for them and what isn't, i.e. requesting feedback, reviewing progress on goals, etc.

4   *The coach is a professional and can be relied upon*: a coach will often encourage high standards of professionalism or integrity from the coachee during coaching conversations, e.g. keeping promises or commitments made. To make that more acceptable, the coach must lead by example. The coach needs to demonstrate that they are a person of integrity, a person of their word. This can be illustrated in simple ways, such as keeping appointments, delivering information or documents promised, etc. When the coach prepares a structured approach to working, this becomes much easier to do.

So it is important that a coach considers these factors before beginning a new assignment and decides how much process and rigour is needed to support that assignment. For example, if a coach has agreed to supply ten general coaching sessions over a six-month period, it makes sense to schedule all ten sessions by mutual agreement from the beginning. A good coach will probably want to plan their approach over the course of sessions, e.g. What performance measures are possible? What might be appropriate points at which to give or receive feedback?

Alternatively, if a coachee wants only two sessions around a specific area or situation, then spending time agreeing lots of principles of approach and guidelines may confuse the coachee, or get in the way of the coaching conversations. The coach must then consider what is the minimum structure needed for the sessions, to create a balance and focus within each session.

Four stages of a coaching assignment

It is possible to identify four key activities or stages that effectively support a series of coaching sessions. These stages are shown in Fig. 4.1.

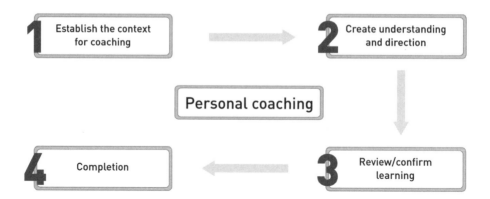

Fig. 4.1 Four stages of a coaching assignment

Some of these stages will often happen naturally, while others require the coach to make them happen. I find that most coaching assignments are more effective when I work with these stages as a foundation.

Whilst a series of coaching sessions will never develop according to a prepared formula, I find that working within a flexible framework still feels useful. Additionally, it is easier for me to demonstrate to a client that they are buying a quality service that has some robust thinking and principles as a foundation. It's natural that people want to balance investment with real results, or the probability of results. The stages or activities that follow can support that conversation, by demonstrating a clear focus on achieving the coachee's outcomes.

A set of four developing activities

Once begun, the four activities are like plates that must be kept spinning. For example, throughout the assignment the coach will always be developing understanding and maintaining direction, constantly reviewing progress in some way, etc. Much of this happens naturally, with little additional effort from the coach.

So the following begins to build a picture of the various activities and stages of a coaching assignment. (For the purposes of this discussion, I am assuming that a coaching assignment is between three and ten sessions long.)

Stage one – establish the context for coaching

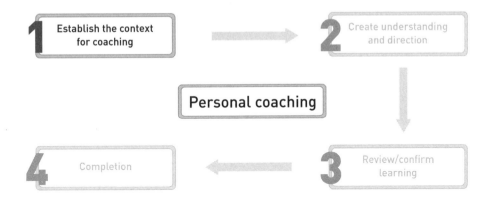

First, we must build a supporting context within which to coach. By context, I mean anything surrounding the actual coaching conversations that might help or hinder those conversations. This might be anything from physical aspects, such as the room, lighting, etc. to non-physical aspects, such as the awareness of the coachee of what's happening, their enthusiasm, etc. This is key to an effective coaching process, in that we are forming expectations, ground rules and awareness that we will use throughout the coaching relationship. Once these principles are formed, they create a foundation upon which subsequent coaching conversations can be built.

Conversely, too much scene setting can be counterproductive to the coaching experience. Part of what happens in coaching can only be described as magical, and too much discussion of these aspects in advance can simply spoil the surprise. If the coach explains the possibility of amazing insights, wonderful events or mind-blowing breakthroughs, then the secret is spoilt, isn't it? Worse, the coach might over-promise on results that aren't delivered – which benefits no one.

Let's now look in more detail at some factors that can contribute to building a great context within which to coach.

Make sure the physical environment supports coaching

Here, we must make sure the room is quiet enough, private enough, and suited to coaching conversations. Are the chairs comfortable enough, is there a table if we want one? Do we have other facilities available to us to enable some flexibility within the session?

Both parties need to feel positive about working within the surroundings.

For example, flip charts, white boards, drinking water, paper, pens, etc. all help spontaneity during the coaching session. Maybe an idea is easier to understand when it's drawn as a picture, maybe the coachee is being distracted because they're thirsty. Both parties need to feel positive about working within the surroundings. If all we've got is a room and two chairs we can easily create the impression of an interrogation room rather than a place to relax and talk freely.

Ideally, a room to be used for coaching sessions should be comfortable and not too cosy – it's important that people can both relax *and* stay alert. Also, the size of the room should create a subtle sense of warmth or intimacy. If the room is very large, the coach and coachee may feel 'lost' in the space or end up sitting too far away from each other. As a balance, if the room is too small, the space can feel awkward and the coach and coachee may have to sit unnaturally close to each other.

Make sure the mechanics of coaching are mutually agreed

Here, we make sure that both the coach and the coachee have agreed the basic facts of the coaching sessions, for example:

➡ Schedule/dates of coaching sessions.

➡ Start and end time of coaching sessions.

➡ Location of coaching sessions.

➡ Who else might be involved in the coaching, e.g. their manager, other coaches, etc.

If the scheduling information is available before the sessions start, it's probably good practice to share this with the coachee in advance of the coaching session. That way, the coachee can put all the sessions into their diary immediately. As well as the obvious practical benefit of securing appointments, the coachee is also encouraged to begin thinking more about the coaching, and what the sessions might bring. Even by writing the coaching sessions into their diary, the coachee becomes more engaged in the future process, as they imagine the journey ahead. Also, the coachee is likely to work between sessions more effectively if they understand when the next one is.

In any instance, I recommend that this information is typed up/photocopied so that both the coach and the coachee have exactly the same information. Misunderstandings at this point may easily lead to either person showing up late or not at all for sessions. If the venue or meeting room is going to change during the ongoing sessions, make sure that's really clear. It's ridiculously easy to have two people sitting in different meeting rooms, each waiting for the other person to show up!

Coach's corner

Q I'm a busy manager – how am I going to schedule regular sessions?

This is a common situation, where a manager is trying to run a busy operation plus make time to coach colleagues and team members. If this is you, please consider the following questions:

- **Q** What are the benefits you will get from coaching others, both personally and professionally?

- **Q** What are reasonable (and still challenging) goals to set for your coaching?

- **Q** What other situations give you an opportunity to develop coaching skills, e.g. questioning, helping others find their own solutions, supportive feedback etc.?

- **Q** How flexible can your coachee be around a coaching schedule, e.g. sessions at short notice?

- **Q** How can you create more time to coach? (Make a list!)

I would encourage any manager to think flexibly and creatively to create more opportunities to coach. Many conversations between managers and colleagues have the potential for some coaching type of input (many of the exercises in this book are based on this simple principle). Rewards over time include colleagues who are more effective, make better decisions and solve their own problems! So if you are a busy manager, and you'd like more time and less pressure – get coaching!

Is the coachee aware of what to expect?

Here, we make sure that the coachee appreciates what coaching is, how it generally works, and what they might expect during the coaching sessions. For example, they need to understand that coaching is not training, and that this kind of learning happens in a different way to training. They need to know that you'll be encouraging them to gain insights, ideas and perspectives on situations that will enable them to act differently, and get different results. They need to know that you will encourage them to focus consistently on their desired goals or outcomes, as a way of maintaining an effective course of action.

I will sometimes give coachees a written overview of what coaching is, broadly how it works, and what I'll be expecting of them (see Appendix 1). If possible, I like to do that in advance of the session, giving the coachee the opportunity to read and digest the information. This works especially well where the coaching engagement is going to be fairly brief, e.g. 1–3 sessions. Additionally, some people welcome reading material as a way of preparing for a coaching relationship.

The key is to find a balance of background information and discussion that is going to enrol and engage the individual. A combination of both documents and discussion up front often helps, enabling the coachee to orient to, and benefit from, the experience.

The following identifies the key elements of a coaching overview:

Coach's toolkit	Coaching overview – key points

What does it do?
➡ Gives someone an initial understanding of coaching, what it is, possible benefits, etc.

➡ Encourages a coachee to begin thinking about any goals or objectives they might have.

When might I use it?
➡ During initial discussions about the potential of coaching.

➡ In advance of the first coaching session.

➡ When beginning a new coaching relationship, to give a new coachee some background information or reading.

What does it cover?
➡ A brief description of what coaching is.

➡ How coaching works, e.g. compared with other forms of learning or training.

➡ What situations might be suited to coaching, and what are the typical benefits.

➡ What the coachee can expect from their coach, e.g. behaviours.

➡ What the coach will expect from the coachee.

➡ Questions that begin to engage the reader, e.g. How might coaching benefit you? What goals or objectives are you focused on? What would you like to change, do more of, etc.?

Taking notes

If you expect the coachee to take their own notes, then they need to know that they're responsible for that. They also need to know that you'll be taking your own notes, and intend to re-read them before each session. This demonstrates both commitment and professionalism from the coach. In addition, it's a practical way of ensuring continuity between each session.

Because I type my own notes up afterwards, I sometimes offer to send a coachee a copy of my own notes, as an additional support for their learning. This can be a valuable discipline for both the coachee and myself. For me, I can mentally review what happened during the session as I'm typing it up. That helps me consider the discussion, my approach and other possible perspectives on the situation. For the coachee, they get to read someone else's view of what happened, perhaps remembering a thought or idea they might not have done otherwise. I also make sure that I record any agreements made, so they can be reviewed during the next session.

I would also balance any recommendation to take notes with another that says don't take too many! Some coaches tend to take too many notes, perhaps because they are anxious not to miss anything. Unfortunately, when a coach is writing notes their ability to observe or listen to the coachee is usually impaired. I tend to write brief 'memory-joggers' and then add other points from memory when I type the notes up afterwards. Alternatively, if the coachee stops speaking to write some of the conversation down, I sometimes use that opportunity to record a point.

Another option is to audiotape the session and then give the tape to the coachee. The coachee might play this in the car, or at home, to review the session. This can also be a useful way of continuing learning, even after the assignment has come to an end. Of course, both the coach and the coachee need to be comfortable with this first.

By various means, the coach and the coachee need to find a good, practical way of recording key information from sessions. In order to maintain both continuity and learning, it's important that both have an accurate picture of broadly what happened and what actions were agreed on.

Engage the coachee in coaching

When we begin to build the context for coaching, we are also beginning the process of engagement. By engagement, we simply mean that the individual is interested, involved, and actively part of what's going on. If an individual isn't engaged in the experience of being coached, then they are much less likely to enjoy and benefit from it. When a coachee is really engaged, they are completely committed to getting the most from the experience. I would say that the more engaged an individual is, the more coachable they become. When someone is coachable, they are more receptive to new ideas and fresh perspectives – they are eager to learn.

I would say that the more engaged an individual is, the more coachable they become.

For the coach, the difference between coaching someone who's engaged in the thought of being coached versus someone who's not engaged or 'bought-in' can mean the difference between fabulous results and no results. Consequently, a coach must carefully consider factors that might affect the coachee's openness to being coached, both before beginning to coach them and during the initial stages of an assignment. The following checklist helps us focus on this a little more.

Checklist   **Signs that the coachee is engaged in the coaching**

➡ The coachee's levels of enthusiasm for the conversation, e.g. energy, ideas, questioning etc., all suggest active engagement.

➡ How active the coachee is between sessions, e.g. completing actions, reading background material to the coaching, even over-performing on agreements or commitments made.

➡ Level of openness in discussion, positive comments or questions, willingness to consider fresh approaches or ideas.

I would also acknowledge that if any or all the above are missing, then that doesn't automatically mean that the individual is not engaged! This is tricky, but nevertheless true. Some people learn and respond differently, and some people become more engaged over time. Patience and flexibility from the coach are needed.

The coach must view each coachee as an individual. Some people are unlikely to respond positively to coaching in the first few sessions. They may by nature be initially cautious in their response to anything new. This might display itself as reluctance to discuss certain situations, hesitation when changing behaviours or even a challenging attitude towards the coach. The coach must balance a commitment to create progress and learning, with sensitivity towards the coachee's way of learning.

We can now look in more detail at those factors that might affect an individual's sense of engagement.

Does the coachee want the coaching?

If someone has requested, and paid for, coaching, we can usually assume that they want the coaching. This becomes less straightforward when coaching within business, as the coachee may not have asked for it, and is not paying for it. Indeed, the coachee in that situation may resent being coached. Where a different person or department has enlisted the coach's services, it is important to spend time making sure the individual is happy being coached, and aware of the opportunity that being coached presents to them.

Where an individual has been requested by their manager to attend some coaching sessions, they might easily be sceptical and/or mistrustful of what this means for them. They might imagine coaching is happening because of a problem with their behaviour that they aren't aware of. Or they may wonder if the coaching sessions are actually some kind of 'vetting' activity, e.g. for redundancy or promotion. They may be concerned that whatever they say during coaching is reported back to their manager or colleagues.

When the coachee has not requested the coaching, I make it a practice to encourage the requesting manager to spend time explaining the arrangement and the reasons for it. I normally request that the manager brief the coachee personally, in advance of my first session. Whilst I can tell the coachee why I think they are having coaching, what they really want is to hear this from the manager. If it's possible, I would encourage any coach to sit in on the session between the manager and the coachee. That way they can help the conversation to be effective, by asking questions or clarifying comments. In addition, the coach also gets to see the manager and the coachee together, which may provide useful insights into that relationship.

What does the coachee expect to happen?

If what begins to happen in the coaching is not what the coachee was expecting, this can cause them discomfort. For example, do they know what sort of approach the coach is going to use in the coaching? If they're expecting magical answers or knowledge to be given to them by the coach, this can lead to silent frustration and disillusionment during sessions. This might easily disappear over time, as they become aware of the benefits of a non-directive approach. More preferable is that they are open to this approach from the very beginning of the sessions.

Negative expectations may arise when the individual has a poor view of coaching, based on previous experiences. For example, maybe they work within an environment where individuals are regularly critical of each other and call this coaching or feedback. A colleague may have been highly critical of them and told them to view it as 'coaching'. Not surprisingly, a potential coachee with this type of experience might not welcome an offer of coaching on a regular basis.

Managing these expectations can be helped both by the coaching overview document (see Appendix 1), and by the coach discussing expectations at the initial coaching sessions.

Does the individual really want change?

This is a similar point to whether they want the coaching, but subtly different. Some people say they want coaching, involve themselves in a coaching relationship, attend sessions, join in conversations – and don't actually want anything to change. It is not uncommon for us to have problems that we don't want to solve, simply because by solving them, we see that we could end up with what seems like a bigger problem.

For example, I might say I hate my job with its lack of responsibility and low salary. I might spend a long time describing why it's so awful, and what kind of job I'd really like to be doing. Between coaching sessions, however, I might do nothing. Each coaching visit, my coach listens to my complaints and wonders why I'm not acting from the insights and decisions I appear to be experiencing.

The answer possibly lies in the fact that I never completely wanted the change. You see, to go and get a better, more responsible, higher paid job might confront my ability to actually do the job. Alternatively, I've been discussing a subject that's easy for me to explore, and non-confronting in nature. I may have other issues that are more challenging, but I'm simply not up for talking about them.

This is another opportunity for the coach to use their advanced skills of supportive feedback! Here, the coach needs to be open and honest about what they think is happening, i.e. a reluctance to embrace change. This enables them to explore what might be causing the apparent block, and appreciate the coachee's views on what's happening. Together, the coach and coachee must find ways to create progress. It might mean that the coachee needs to consider what they really want more fully, or perhaps how they're stopping themselves from having it.

Coach's toolkit	Does someone want change?

What is this? ➡ A way to help you to evaluate a coachee's appetite for change.

What does it do? ➡ Causes you to reflect on how receptive the coachee is to learning and change.

When might I use it? ➡ In the early stages of a coaching assignment.

➡ At any point during a coaching assignment when you consider that a reluctance to change may be a reason for little or no progress.

Consider the following questions:

Q During sessions, to what extent does the coachee demonstrate enthusiasm for acquiring new thoughts, e.g. seeking other ways of doing things, 'What could I do to change that?' 'What would I need to do?'

Q During sessions, does the coachee prefer to discuss problems rather than solutions?

Q Between sessions, how 'in action' is the coachee, e.g. do they complete agreements, use new behaviours, continue to learn, read, do their own research, etc.?

> **Toolkit Summary**   **Does someone want change?**
>
> There are many reasons for a coachee not to appear engaged in the coaching, and not really wanting to change is just one. Later in this chapter we look at another, more structured approach to this situation.

Begin to focus on desired outcomes

When building context, we also begin to explore what the coachee wants to get from the series of coaching sessions. I would hope to start this enquiry before the first session takes place. Using the coaching overview document, the coach can suggest that the coachee consider what their goals might be, and what situations or issues currently relate to those goals.

By helping the coachee to begin thinking in this way, the coach helps the coachee to enter the initial session with a sense of preparation. Perhaps they've thought a little more about what areas of their life or work they want to work on, or simply have some questions based on the information they've been given.

Also, by encouraging the coachee to imagine the future series of coaching sessions – what might happen, etc. – the coach is also initiating the learning process. This is sometimes called 'future pacing'. When we 'future pace' someone's thoughts we are beginning to engage them in their future, helping them imagine what's going to happen before it actually does. For example, if I want to future pace your goal of losing weight and becoming much more healthy, I'm going to encourage you to imagine what having that goal will be like. That would include how you would look, how you would feel, how your experiences of life would be different – a really rich appreciation of what losing weight and being healthy would be like.

Future pacing is a valuable technique within any change process, as it has the effect of drawing someone's mind towards having a goal. This has both a practical and motivational result. By really thinking through what the goal of health and weight loss would be like, we begin to identify any practical issues with that. Maybe I don't actually want to lose as much weight as I thought, and by imagining myself this much lighter I can see that clearly.

Also, when I imagine myself looking slimmer and fitter I can become quite inspired by how that might feel and look – and that's going to motivate me to have my goal even more.

The same principles apply when an individual begins to imagine what benefits they might experience from being coached. Harnessing the power of the coachee's imagination begins to create a strong 'pulling' effect towards a desirable future.

Coach's corner

Q **That's all great but how do I actually start off my first coaching session?**

It is important to start off any initial conversation with a coachee on a firm footing. With a little advance preparation or thought this becomes fairly simple. As you prepare, perhaps consider:

Q What do I want to get out of this first session?

Q How will I know that the session has been a success?

Q What might stop the session from being a success?

Q What do I want the coachee's experience to be?

Q What simple principle or belief do I want to remember during the session?

For further help, see the checklist: How much structure do I need? (p. 101)

Relax the conversation, gain rapport

Introduce yourself if necessary, i.e. if you've not met before. Lighten the situation a little by discussing something familiar and easy to them, e.g. something about the company, their colleagues, maybe your journey (and if you're really stuck there's always the weather!).

Check that the coachee is orientated to the conversation

Make sure they've had all the information they need as background, e.g. 'Did you have a chance to read the coaching overview – was that helpful?' Explain what's going to happen in this first session, e.g. 'So I'm hoping to spend the next couple of hours getting to know a little bit more about you and what you'd like to get out of coaching – is that OK?'

Gently get to know them

Take some personal details down (where they live, if they have children etc.), e.g. 'Can I ask you a few basic facts so I know a little more about you.' This is an obvious place to create some more easy conversation, e.g. take a genuine interest in what they're telling you, ask a little bit more about their home life etc.

Gently explore what they think they'd like to get from the coaching

If some of these goals are already known, then acknowledge them, e.g. 'You mentioned on the phone that you'd like to focus on being more organized, could you perhaps tell me a little more about that?' If no goals have been discussed yet start with something gentle like 'What kinds of things were you thinking of working on?' Sometimes the coachee either doesn't know or isn't comfortable enough to discuss goals yet. In this instance, simply have a general discussion, e.g. 'Perhaps begin then by telling me a little more about yourself' or 'OK, can you tell me a little more about what you do at work?'

Once you've found something that they are comfortable discussing, that's it, you're off! You can then use all your skills of listening, questioning, observation and feedback to begin to support their learning and development.

If you are interested in seeing a narrative of a full coaching session, use the following link: www.business-minds.com/go to/coachingmanual

Stage two – create understanding and direction

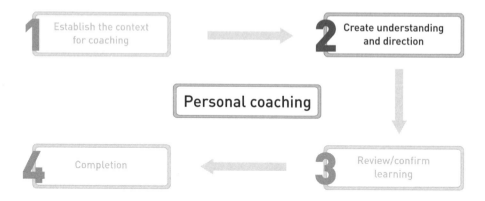

The second stage of a coaching assignment places a stronger emphasis on what the coachee wants to achieve within the coaching whilst identifying where they are right now. Once understanding and a sense of direction have been established, these can be developed throughout all sessions.

Getting to know the coachee

Initially, the coach needs to form an appropriate level of understanding of the coachee as a person, their current circumstances, issues, etc. This information gathering will ideally begin before the coach and coachee sit down to a coaching session. Before I begin any new coaching conversation, I like to know:

➡ The coachee's full name.

➡ Their age.

➡ What they do for a job/occupation.

➡ Where they live and where they work (and the type of journey between).

➡ Family circumstances, partner's name, number, names and age of children.

➡ What general areas they would like to work with, e.g. confidence, productivity, health, or finances.

Some of that seems personal and asking for such information on a form or over the telephone seems inappropriate. I tend to gather the most basic details before the session, i.e. name, occupation and perhaps areas they want to work on. Then at the beginning of the first session, I ask for the other information, family, where they live/work, etc. People are sometimes surprised that I'm interested in knowing their partner's name, where they live, or even how long they've been married. However, most people happily accept that all these factors have a potential influence on the work we are embarking upon.

For example, perhaps in the second session we are discussing a recent job offer. I would want to understand the impact this might have on the coachee's home or family life and, at that point, it's better for me to be able to ask 'And what does Rachel think about this?' than 'Can I ask, are you married?'

Both for the flow of conversation, and the sense of a relationship between the coach and coachee, it pays to have some basic knowledge of a coachee's life and circumstances upon which to build.

Getting to know what the coachee wants

From the first session, we need to begin agreeing what areas of their life the coachee wants to change or improve on and what specific goals they might have in those areas. This begins the ongoing process of keeping a focus on those goals or desired outcomes. These stated goals and aims form the basis for each coaching conversation. The goals may change, or be refined, but a coach must always keep the coachee's goals as the background for the sessions.

Without this constant focus, coaching conversations can develop into cosy chats, with no real purpose or sense of direction. The coach and the coachee may update themselves on what's been happening with the coachee, what was interesting about that, enjoyable or frustrating, etc. The point is, with no underlying goal or sense of direction, this is just a cosy chat. Not that there's anything wrong with cosy chats, I love them – they're just not coaching!

Maintaining direction within each session

The need to establish purpose and direction is also important within each session. At the beginning of each session, a good coach will often want to set a target for the coachee, e.g. 'What do you want to achieve in today's session?' By agreeing on expectations, the coach can review progress against that target if the discussion is drifting, e.g. 'We said we wanted to find ways of creating more time for your children today – are you happy that we continue with this discussion of promotion at work?'

The coach needs to find ways to maintain progress, and stay flexible as to the natural flow of the coaching discussions.

The coach needs to find ways to maintain progress, and stay flexible as to the natural flow of the coaching discussions. Sometimes, the coaching conversation that occurs seems unrelated to any of the coachee's goals, but a good coach may choose to continue. This is when experience and intuition tell the coach that the conversation that's happening is valuable and worthwhile. In these cases, such conversations can prove incredibly relevant to the coachee's overall progress and are easily worth the digression.

Using the previous example – by discussing the promotion at work, the coachee may realize that the price she's paying for career success is often her relationship with her children. She may decide that she needs to find ways of balancing these different aspects of fulfilment and happiness.

Developing goals

So when a coach begins working with a new coachee, it makes sense to develop a good understanding of what the individual wants to work on during the forthcoming sessions. For example, if the coachee wants to get a better job or career, both the coach and the coachee need to understand:

➡ What specifically does 'better job' mean? Is that defined by an increase in salary, benefits, responsibility, working conditions, job content, working location, job title, training, etc.? The possibilities for how a coachee might decide a job is better than the one they have right now are endless.

➡ What circumstances currently relate to that goal, e.g. money problems, frustrations with current employer, contractual obligations, notice period, etc.?

➡ What are the coachee's reasons (motivators) for wanting the goal, e.g. financial security/freedom, lifestyle, personal profile, respect, etc.?

➡ What might stop, or form a barrier to, the coachee achieving this goal, e.g. fear of change/risk, academic qualifications/work experience, peer pressure, etc.?

Often, just discussing what a coachee actually wants and defining that with real clarity can be of tremendous benefit. By creating a richer appreciation of the motivators, circumstances and issues that are involved in a person's goals, we can often create an immediate shift in their perception. It is not uncommon for a coachee to have a complete change of heart about what they want, when they gain this richer understanding.

Coach's story

A male coachee tells the coach in the initial session that he wants to focus some of the sessions on finding ways to support his son's education. The coachee is frustrated at his son's lack of progress in some key subjects (in particular, maths) and wants to consider other options, e.g. private tuition, changing schools etc. The coach then spends time exploring the situation a little more. The coach looks not only at what the coachee says he wants to provide for his son, i.e. a good education, but also at what might be causing the coachee's frustration or what values the coachee is operating from.

From the discussion, the coachee realizes that he doesn't actually mind that his son is no good at maths. After all, he is excelling in other areas that come more naturally to him. What frustrates the coachee is that his son is very relaxed about the situation, and isn't visibly worried or stressed about it. The son loves English, history and sports, and views maths as something to be 'tolerated'. This contrasts with the coachee's upbringing, where a strict father took all education very seriously, and encouraged the coachee to worry a lot about any areas where he might be 'failing'.

The coachee realizes that he does not want to teach his son to worry, or become stressed about circumstances such as his lack of natural ability for maths. The coachee recognizes that what he's really committed to is supporting his son to live an enjoyable and productive life, one that fulfils him. Strangely, the coachee now views his son as someone he can learn from, in terms of his responses to situations. He finds he actually admires the way his son can really enjoy the things he's good at, and find pleasure at being good at something. Conversely, his son can also deal with things he's not good at, and view them in a relaxed way.

This is quite a shift in perception for the coachee, who tends to disregard all his own successes and worries instead about the areas in his life where he thinks he's 'failing'.

By exploring the coachee's goals fully, the coach is able to reach this conclusion fairly quickly. In addition, the coachee now has a new goal that will really benefit him, i.e. learning a new, relaxed way of being from his son.

Goals within any coaching assignment are essential to success. It follows then that the goal should be defined and understood in a way that enables both the coach and the coachee to create forward movement and progress.

Coach's toolkit	Building a clear goal	

What is this?	➡ A way of helping someone define a goal or objective they have more clearly.
What does it do?	➡ Helps someone gain a fuller understanding of their goal.
	➡ Explores the motivation behind their goal.

> ➡ Either (a) increases their motivation towards their goal, or (b) helps them realize they don't really want it after all!

> ➡ Identifies situations or barriers that might stop them from having their goal.

> ➡ Agrees immediate actions related to the goal.

When might I use it? ➡ During initial coaching sessions, when discussing what goals the coachee wants to work on.

> ➡ Any time that someone seems to have a vague goal or 'wish', e.g. 'I wish I had a better job'.

> ➡ Parts of it may also be used in isolation, e.g. some questions work well on their own in general conversation.

Learning guidelines

The stages described below deal with those aspects of the goal that need to be explored and discussed by the coach. The aspects can be covered in the order in which they are written here, or in a different sequence if desired. It's more important to create a conversation that flows naturally. I find the best way to learn these aspects is to first write a checklist, e.g. make a note of the headings, then tick each one when you've covered it. Pretty soon you'll remember them and be able to hold the conversation naturally without the list.

Some stages might be covered quickly, whilst others require further discussion. For example, someone might know exactly what they want, but need help understanding why they want it.

The 'Coaching questions' are suggestions you might find useful. Simply use those questions that work for you and the situation you are discussing. Remain flexible throughout the conversation, e.g. if the person changes their mind as to what they want. When this happens, you may have to go back a few steps to create a clear view of the revised goal.

State the goal in positive terms

The goal must always be stated in terms of what the individual **wants**, rather than what they don't want, for example:

What they don't want: 'Stop losing my temper so often.'
What they *do* want: 'Keep calm and relaxed in difficult situations.'

Coaching questions – be positive

'What **do** you want?'
'What would you rather have or be true?'
'What do you want instead?'
'What is it you actually **do** want?'

Get specific! What, where, when, with whom?

In order to be really clear about the goal, we begin to add more and more detail. For example, 'I want more energy' is too vague. We need to understand when, where and with whom, e.g. 'I want more energy to be able to play sports with my kids after work.' If there's a timescale involved, find out what it is, e.g. within three months.

Coaching questions – be specific

'When do you want more energy specifically?'
'Is there some activity or time you'd especially like more energy for?'
'How much more energy?'
'With whom?'
'When?'
'Where?'
'Which situations do you want more energy in?'

Remember to focus on what **they** want, and not what *you* think would be good, e.g.
'Wouldn't it be better to play sports with your kids at the weekend?'

You may sometimes want to challenge the person a little, either to improve the goal, or their level of commitment. Please use care and judge wisely if you do. The person will normally understand what is a stretch for them. Sometimes a simple question will identify whether the goal is challenging enough, e.g. 'How much of a challenge is that for you?'

Use the senses to pull it closer

Using other senses, e.g. sight, sound, etc. helps the individual to create images or ways of representing the goal, to enable them to understand the goal more easily. It is even more powerful to ask these questions from a position of assuming they already have the goal.

Coaching questions – pull it closer

'How will you **know** when you have your dream job?'

'Imagine you have your dream job – what do you feel like?'

'How are things different now that you have your dream job?'

'How does this affect the way you look?'

'What are people saying about you now that you have this dream job?'

'So, imagine you have this dream job – now tell me what that's like.'

Is this your goal – or someone else's?

A goal is more easily reached when it is within the natural influence of the individual who wants it. For example, I can't get my boss or partner to stop acting stressed around me, but I can have the goal of responding in a relaxed, resourceful way to their behaviour. I can control my own actions – not those of others. I can't have a goal for someone else. Also, when someone else has a goal for me, I need to want it as well in order to be really motivated to make it happen.

So we need to discuss the goal in a way which establishes a clear responsibility, or influence, over the goal.

Coaching questions – check influence

'How much influence do you have over this?'

'Are you responsible for making your goal happen?'

'What can you do to achieve it?'

'Is it within your power to influence this?'

'Who else wants this for you?'

A question of balance

We want to make sure that it's 'OK' for the individual to have this goal, in relation to the rest of their life. For example, if someone wants to travel more with their job, and they have young children, they need to look at the effect of travel upon their home life. By exploring the impact of their goal on other situations, we work to maintain balance. We are also respecting other parts of their life, people and things around them, by considering any negative effects elsewhere.

Coaching questions – check balance

'What would the consequences of getting this goal be?'

'Are there any negative consequences of having this?'

'How would having this affect your home life (or your family, or your friends)?'

'How does this affect other people at work?'

'How does this affect other things which are important to you?'

Increase motivation

This is a way of referring to basic values, and understanding our goal in relation to those values. By aligning with values that are important to us, we can better understand the priority of our goal. For example, if variety and challenge are important to you, you may notice that it doesn't 'feel good' to consider doing exactly the same job for the next three years. However, if security and stability are more important to you, you may view three years in the same job as perfect.

In this check we also identify potential barriers, either internal or external, in order to shift those barriers.

Coaching questions – increase motivation

'What would achieving this do for you?'
'What higher purpose does this fulfil?'
'If you have this, what sort of person will that make you?'
'What else will you get if you have this?'
'What is stopping you from having this?'
'What might stop you from having this?'
'As you think about the journey towards this – what might stand in your way?'
'If you could have this right now – would you take it?'

That final question is a clever one, as it works with people's gut instinct. Ask someone who says they want to quit smoking that question, e.g. 'If I could make you a non-smoker right now – would you let me?' If they hesitate, that's usually because they have some doubt. Once you've identified the hesitation, you can explore the cause.

Taking action – do it now!

This check identifies the next logical action in relation to the goal, and gains commitment to taking this action. We begin to move out of thinking and talking about it, and into 'doing'. For example, 'I want to study for my degree' becomes 'I'm going to call three colleges to get their current syllabus'. You may choose to support the individual further by gaining a more formal agreement to taking this action, e.g. which colleges, by when – and agree to check in later to hear what progress has been made.

Coaching questions – taking action

'What can you do to achieve this goal?'
'What is the next/first step for you now?'
'What's the next logical thing you would do to achieve this?'

'What one (or two, or three) thing (s) could you be doing right now which would have tremendous impact on your progress towards this goal?'

Toolkit Summary   **Building a clear goal**

By talking through different perspectives on their goal, the individual will normally benefit. Hopefully they will be feeling clearer, optimistic, and perhaps more determined or motivated as a result.

Alternatively, they might have discarded the original goal completely, having realized that it wasn't something that they really wanted or would benefit from. Maybe they've replaced it with a new goal, or maybe they need to go away and do some more 'thinking'. In either instance, the coach now knows much more about the person's thinking, and can support them more effectively.

Using personality profiling or 360° feedback

Developing an understanding of the individual can be greatly enhanced by the use of personality profiling and/or 360° feedback. These tests consist of a series of structured questions used to assess characteristics of an individual. The characteristics assessed will depend on what kind of test is used, e.g. creativity, thinking patterns etc. Standard tests like these have a fairly objective approach, i.e. using the same test, each person would be asked exactly the same questions. The results give another view of an individual than that normally gained during coaching discussions. For example, a coach might ask a coachee if they are creative and they may answer 'not really', as they don't think of themselves as creative in any way. When assessed using a standard test, the answers given may suggest that the individual is in fact highly creative. Unless an individual is doing a job or role that is obviously creative, e.g. artist, poet, they might easily assume they are not. The individual may not realize the creativity involved in what they already do, e.g. finding solutions to problems. The alternative views provided by tests can really improve understanding and progress within the coaching.

Personality profiling

Personality tests examine our individual character traits from a completely independent/objective view. Normally, we fill in a form, and our responses are analyzed to give us some results. The results might point to what we like, what we don't like, what kind of jobs we'd be really good at, how we typically approach problems, etc. There are many different types of test – too many to discuss here. Some popular examples are Myers-Briggs, the LAB or Belbin, all of which can also be used to understand teams, as well as individuals.

Some tests focus on certain qualities, e.g. of leadership, whilst others are much more general, e.g. are we creative, are we a 'people person' etc. Personality tests are useful as they can help a coachee discuss themselves and their typical behaviours in a much less emotional or attached manner. No one can be right or wrong in a personality test, as there are no good or bad personality types. In addition, it can help the coach learn to relate to the coachee in a way that the coachee will naturally respond to. For example, if the coach knows that a coachee likes to learn by reading, they can offer book recommendations.

360° feedback

360° feedback is subtly different, as people who know the coachee, plus the coachee themselves, fill in the questionnaires. Within business, the coachee's colleagues, manager, and people who work for them might all complete forms. Again, the questions involved might be general or very specific, e.g. 'Are they influential?' or 'How much does this person show enthusiasm?'

When a coachee gets this kind of feedback, it can be very powerful for them, as they rarely have this view of themselves through the eyes of others. How other people experience them may not be as they imagined. So getting this feedback can lead to breakthroughs in a coachee's understanding. For example, a coachee is frustrated with her lack of acknowledgement or promotion at work. When her 360° feedback is returned, she gains information that helps her understand why. Her manager and colleagues view her as happy, contented, and unambitious. In addition, she is viewed as someone who prefers a small group of colleagues and does not actively seek new friends or contacts. By receiving this feedback, the coachee is encouraged to actively promote herself and her objectives, by developing more relationships with a much broader group of people.

Both personality tests and 360° feedback require the coach to be very good at giving feedback. The information these tests produce should be experienced by the coachee as valuable, stimulating and worthwhile. This requires the coach to devote time and energy to delivering the results of the 360° feedback in a supportive, sensitive manner. For further information, please refer to the supportive feedback section of coaching core skills in Chapter 5.

In summary, I would say that profiling tools are a valuable addition to any coach's set of skills. They create the opportunity for a different type of conversation, which can create a clearer understanding and direction for the coaching assignment.

An exercise   **Find out more about profiling**

I invite you to find out more about the opportunities of personality profiling. Here are some links you might use:

➡ http://www.psychtests.com

➡ http://www.fordham.edu/aps

➡ http://www.minddata.com/history.asp

Alternatively, just type the words 'personality profiling' or 'psychometric testing' into your web browser. If you're interested in books, there are lots! Try your favourite on-line bookseller e.g. amazon.co.uk, waterstones.co.uk or simply visit your local bookstore.

Ongoing development of direction and goals

Once an initial direction and understanding are established, they must be developed throughout the coaching assignment. Understanding is one of the keys to the coachee's development, and coaching discussions are a constant process of enquiry, insight, conclusion and so forth. It's an ongoing journey of discovery and learning, for both the

Success is reached by staying committed to the destination, and flexible as to the journey.

coachee and the coach. Success is reached by staying committed to the destination, and flexible as to the journey. This is why the skills of careful listening and questioning are so important to a good coach.

Stage three – review/confirm learning

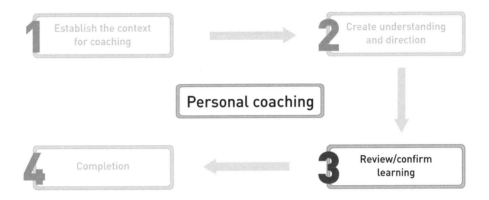

Regular reviews are desirable to maintain good progress within an ongoing coaching assignment. A good coach will be interested in both the effectiveness of the coaching sessions, and whether or not the coachee is making good progress in achieving their goals. During a review activity, we might explore any or all of the following:

➡ Are the coaching sessions working well, e.g. are they productive, worthwhile, etc.?

➡ What impact are the sessions having on the coachee?

➡ What progress has been made on the coachee's goals?

➡ Is the coach's style and approach working for the coachee?

➡ Are there any issues that need to be resolved, e.g. what's not working?

➡ How could the sessions be improved?

If the above questions appear to be intended only for the coachee, that's not strictly true. Mostly it is the coachee who places a value upon the coaching, as they are the focal point of the conversations, and the person who should be benefiting from them. However, the coach will also have views on all of the above, as well as other coaching experience to draw upon. In addition, the coach may have their own goals within the coaching, such as improving their listening or rapport skills. It makes sense, therefore, that both the coach and the coachee have the opportunity to give their views.

| Checklist | Ways to review progress of a coaching assignment |

➡ Give the coachee a questionnaire to complete between sessions.

➡ Use a questionnaire to conduct a structured review session with the coachee.

➡ Schedule an unstructured discussion with the coachee to explore the progress of the coaching.

➡ Conduct regular, smaller, reviews with the coachee, e.g. at the end of each session.

➡ Ask for informal feedback from the coachee on an ad hoc basis, e.g. when it seems appropriate.

➡ Arrange for a third party, e.g. another coach, to facilitate a discussion between the coach and the coachee.

➡ Complete a feedback questionnaire on your own experience (as coach).

➡ Arrange a coaching session with another coach to review progress (very useful where you are having some difficulty or issues with the assignment).

Deciding when and how to review

A coach needs to strike a balance between how much time is spent reviewing the coaching, and how much time is spent actually coaching. Too many reviews can easily impair the flow of coaching conversations, causing an unnatural focus on the conversations themselves. Alternatively, if a coach disregards the review process, they risk missing an issue, or an opportunity to improve the effectiveness of the sessions for the coachee. Imagine that you and I were doing a 1,000-piece jigsaw puzzle together. Occasionally, we might step back to review our progress and check everything was going okay. However if we stopped to discuss every little piece going into place we'd slow our progress considerably!

There are no strict guidelines, although I like to schedule at least a couple of formal checks into any coaching assignment more than five sessions long. This might consist of one check around the mid-point of the coaching initiative and one a few weeks after the coaching has finished. The prompt of giving feedback 3–4 weeks after the coaching has finished gives the coachee an opportunity to give a reflective view, based on their experiences after the coaching has ended. In addition, the activity of giving feedback reminds them of the insights and learning they have gained, and perhaps encourages them to apply those lessons a little more rigorously.

In addition, I like to include some informal reviews in the sessions. These will normally consist of a few open questions, to explore how things are with the coachee. Maybe at the beginning or the end of the sessions, I might ask things like, 'Was that conversation useful?', 'Is the coaching what you expected?', 'How are we doing, do you think?' Obviously that's not going to produce good quality feedback but it can give a coach some clues as to an underlying problem. If a coachee answers such a question with an emphatic 'Yes – absolutely' then the coach can assume that there are no major problems. If a coachee pauses, and perhaps with less energy responds 'Yeah – I guess so', then further exploration is probably needed.

Occasionally, I'll also do my own reviews of progress, by re-reading all the notes I've kept on the coachee from the beginning of the sessions.

Table 4.1 shows a typical schedule of reviews over a ten-session coaching assignment.

Other options for reviews include a telephone call between sessions, or maybe an e-mail to check how things are.

If the above appears to create a lot of reviewing, remember, the coachee will really only notice the more formal stages consisting of the two questionnaires. For the coach, much of the above can happen almost subconsciously, e.g. as I'm filing someone's notes, I'll sometimes re-read the others that are there. This will often provoke me to think about what's happening with that coachee generally, and I may choose to do something different in the next session because of that.

Table 4.1 Schedule of reviews over a ten-session coaching assignment

	Nature of review	Comment
Session one	Informal check in at end of session, e.g. 'Was that what you expected?'	Helps match the coachee's expectations to reality.
Session two	Informal check in at beginning of session, e.g. 'How were you after the last session?'. At end of session, quick informal check, e.g. 'Was that a useful discussion to have?'	
Session three	Informal check at end of session, plus coach reviews all notes before next session.	
Session four	Informal checks at start of session, based on coach's view having re-read the notes, e.g. 'Let's have a look at how we've doing so far. I want to do a quick recap using the session notes.'	
Session five	Informal check at end of session, e.g. 'Was that useful?' plus a request that the coachee completes a feedback questionnaire before the next session.	Need to engage the coachee in the value of giving open feedback.
Session six	Acknowledge results of feedback, and discuss any matters arising, e.g. need to alter session times, focus more on work issues, etc.	

Session seven	Informally review what progress is being made on the coachee's goals. Agree what further progress the coachee wants to make before the final session.	This discussion is normally at the beginning of the session.
Session eight	Acknowledge focus of session, i.e. the coachee's goals. Confirm that any review points from structured feedback (Session 6) are now working, e.g. new session times, etc.	
Session nine	Informal checks at end of session, e.g. 'Are we still on track to meet our targets by the next session?' Tell the coachee you'll be reviewing progress more formally next time.	
Session ten	More formal review of progress on goals, record in notes. Give final feedback form for completion after session.	Final feedback form is useful a few weeks after completion, e.g. 3–6 weeks.

Confirming learning

By reviewing the progress and results of coaching, we are able to affirm learning with the coachee. By this affirmation, we are simply linking what the coachee is learning with the benefits they are experiencing as a result. Benefits such as better relationships with others, increased personal productivity, increased health and well-being, etc. By forming a clear link between the coaching and the results of coaching, we achieve several aims, namely:

1   *The coachee realizes the benefit of their commitment to coaching*: the coachee now sees an obvious return on the effort they have put into coaching so far, e.g. trust, openness, completing actions etc.

2   *The coachee is encouraged to develop new behaviours further*: by seeing how much they have benefited from taking on actions or new behaviours, the coachee is motivated to continue, in order to generate more positive results.

3   *The business gains an appreciation of the potential of coaching*: where the coaching has been sponsored by an organization, e.g. a training department or senior manager, they can most likely link the results of coaching to a business benefit. Perhaps the individual has a marked improvement in productivity, or personal effectiveness – these are both results that directly benefit the organization.

Linking results to coaching

There are many ways a coach might choose to assess the results of coaching, for example:

➡   Give the coachee a structured questionnaire, asking them to identify new behaviours and results (this becomes part of the earlier review process).

➡   Have a structured conversation with the coachee, to explore what differences they are noticing (again, forms part of a review process).

➡   Speak to colleagues or friends; ask for feedback on the individual. To maintain trust, the coach must be really open with the coachee about doing this, i.e. ask permission to do this, pass information or comments back to the coachee, etc.

➡   Observe the individual in their workplace or indeed anywhere that seems appropriate to view results, e.g. if they wanted to be better at public speaking, go and watch them do that.

➡   Repeat 360° feedback later with the same group of friends or colleagues, and look at changes in the results from the first exercise.

Obviously the coach needs to appreciate the individual coachee's situation, before deciding how to make these links from coaching to results. It may be that an informal discussion is all that's needed. Alternatively, if from the outset the coach and coachee have agreed on some very specific behavioural changes as goals, then observing (or shadowing) them may be a good idea.

Checklist	Linking coaching to results

The following is a checklist of questions you might use with a coachee to understand the impact of coaching conversations. They are very simple, and you'll probably want to add your own:

Q What benefits do you see from the coaching?

Q What effects are the coaching conversations having on your work/home/relationship etc.? (choose whichever is appropriate)

Q If you hadn't had the coaching – what would be different now?

Q If you continue with these new behaviours and routines, how is the future different? e.g. what impact will this have at work/home etc.?

Q What have you got from the coaching conversations?

What if there aren't any results?

Where the individual is experiencing no results, and neither are friends or colleagues, then noticing this is important. If the coach neglects to identify that the coaching is having no effect, then they have no opportunity to improve the situation. In addition, where the coach works within a business environment, and their sponsor is not the coachee, the sponsor must be happy they are investing time and money wisely.

Sometimes, coaching doesn't produce the results that we hoped it would.

Sometimes, coaching doesn't produce the results that we hoped it would. By identifying that the coaching seems to be having no effect on the individual, the coach is then able to explore that with the coachee. Together, the coach and coachee can look at what's happening, and why, and decide on a course of action if that's appropriate.

What if the results are not good?

Sometimes, an individual experiencing coaching may find that things get worse before they can get better. This is a natural part of the learning cycle and both the coach and the coachee should be prepared for it as a possibility. For example, a coachee is used to getting results at work by using demanding, controlling behaviours. They are used to getting quick results, but find over time colleagues either refuse to help, or simply avoid working with them. The coachee recognizes this and wants to learn other ways of making requests of people, whilst maintaining a good relationship with them.

Now at first the coachee simply stops barking orders at people, as they are now aware of the impact this has been having on their colleagues. As a consequence, important tasks aren't shared, and the coachee is overloaded with work. As coaching continues, the coachee realizes this, and practises new ways of making requests of their colleagues.

The coachee returns to the work environment to try out these new behaviours. It seems it may take a little time for them to find the right balance between making an open request of someone, and maintaining rapport at the same time. Until they learn the best way to do this, they may experience a combination of positive results and lousy results (or results that are somewhere in between).

Stage four – completion

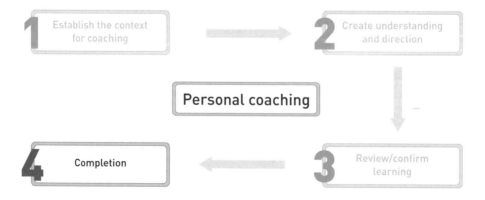

This is logically the final stage of coaching, as its purpose is to bring the coaching assignment to a natural conclusion. No matter how amazing the benefits from the coaching have been or how enjoyable and stimulating the coaching relationship is, each coaching assignment should have an end to it. Just as there's something very exciting about embarking upon the beginning of a coaching initiative, there can also be something wonderfully liberating about ending one.

So whilst an assignment with a coach might easily be extended, I would recommend that it not become a permanent arrangement. A coach acts as a catalyst, bringing fresh perspectives, different ideas and a constant focus to the goals of the coachee. If a coach had regular sessions with the same personal coach for a long period of time, e.g. years, I would expect the value of that coaching to diminish over time. Maybe the relationship becomes too familiar, and so less challenging. Or perhaps the coachee becomes 'immune' to the ideas and conversation of the coach. It's also possible that the coach becomes so used to the typical behaviours and language of the coachee that they almost stop noticing or questioning them.

In addition, the coachee must assume ultimate responsibility for themselves and their circumstances. With the same coach as a constant companion, some of this sense of independence may be lost.

I would also acknowledge that an individual may choose to return to a coaching relationship, for periods where they need a clearer focus or more support over a period of time. I would recommend that individuals consider using different coaches, who have strengths in different areas. I know of coaches who work exclusively in one area, such as time management, or relationships. Depending on the coachee's reasons for returning to coaching, it may be advisable to consider all the available options – there are many good coaches out there.

The purpose of completion

When completing the coaching assignment, the coach aims to:

➡ Leave the coachee feeling that the coaching has been worthwhile. In addition, where someone else has sponsored the coaching, the sponsor should also feel that they have received value from their investment.

➡ Identify ways in which the coachee may continue to learn when the coaching sessions end.

➡ Make sure that the coachee feels they have ways of getting further support if they want it.

It's no good having a wonderful coaching relationship with someone for several months if the coachee is left feeling cast adrift or unsupported a short time after the assignment has ended. We want to encourage the coachee to continue learning, building and developing the insights and ideas that arose during the coaching sessions. That way, the coachee is still getting value long after the last session has ended.

Begin with the end in mind

Strangely, preparing for completion begins right at the beginning of a coaching relationship. The coach must operate from an assumption that the coaching will have an end to it, and that end should fulfil the above criteria. Throughout any coaching assignment, I will be looking for ideas that might support the effective closure of the assignment. For example, I might encourage the individual to create a personal development plan to focus on longer-term learning. Alternatively, I might look for book recommendations or explore possible ways that the coachee may gain more support from individuals that they know or work with.

Leave people feeling good about the coaching

Where the coaching has gone especially well, completion becomes really easy. For the coachee, the review processes have identified benefits, and these have been confirmed. The coachee knows that the coaching has really worked for them, and, specifically, knows **how** it has worked for them. If there was a business sponsor involved, again, the review processes will have identified positive gains for them or the organization.

Where the coaching hasn't achieved the results that were desired or expected, we can use the opportunity of completion to reconcile the situation. For example, additional activities or ideas can be implemented to encourage change. Perhaps the individual requires some training or additional experiences in order to progress. Acknowledging the situation a coach can do something positive about it.

Occasionally a coach will choose to perform a feedback exercise sometime after the coaching has ended. This can be valuable both to confirm benefits and also to pick up any residual issues that need taking care of. For example, if the coach has agreed that the coachee find a friend or colleague to help support their development plan, the coach can hear how this is going on. Maybe this isn't working for the coachee, and they simply need a discussion with the coach to realize why.

Wherever the coachee, or sponsor, is left feeling uncomfortable about some aspects of the coaching, I would hope that the coach would work to resolve that discomfort. Maybe the sponsor was left feeling unclear as to what should happen now, or perhaps the coachee doesn't feel able to take their learning forward. Whatever is incomplete about the coaching will normally be identified, discussed and made complete by a good coach. After all, a coach's success is reflected in what clients and coachees say about them. Most coaches rely on referrals or recommendations for continued business. How a coach handles aspects of review, affirmation and closure within a coaching assignment can have a great impact upon people's impression of their services.

A coach's success is reflected in what clients and coachees say about them.

Personal development plans

A personal development plan identifies areas that the coachee wants to develop further, once the coaching has ended. Goals tend to be over a longer period of time, e.g. months or years, rather than weeks. This might typically include gaining new experience or qualifications, hitting targets of earnings, health, fitness etc. It may also include commitments that the coachee wants to maintain, like using a daily plan, or making a weekly phone call to someone.

Personal development plans are especially useful in business, when used by the coachee to focus specifically on their career development. They form a record for the coachee of the main areas they want to improve in, or goals they want to focus on. Also, these plans can be used to request further training or support from colleagues, managers, training functions etc. Once developmental goals have been met, the plan can be used to demonstrate progress to others. This might be especially important where an organization has a formal appraisal process, where financial reward is linked to performance.

Checklist — Key elements of a personal development plan (PDP)

The following are suggested headings (or columns) within a PDP document:

1   Area of development

This is the general skill or competence, e.g. time management, financial awareness, health/well-being, etc.

2   Development objective (goal)

This is what specifically the individual wants to do, e.g.:

➡ Reduce my working day to eight hours.

➡ Be able to read and understand financial information relating to my project.

➡ Improve my intake of food and drink during working hours.

3   Behaviours to develop and demonstrate competency

This is what the individual will be doing more of, when they start meeting their objective, e.g.:

➡ Use a weekly and daily diary, to prioritize and schedule activity, and review these plans regularly with one other person.

➡ Regularly review financial reports relating to project area, spend compared with budget, etc.

➡ Eat a healthy lunch every day, drink one glass of water for every tea or coffee.

4   Actions to create progress

This is what the individual must do to really get into action on their objective. For example, book on a course, arrange a meeting, find a mentor, etc. Agree on a date by when these arrangements should be completed. Using the three categories above, we might choose:

➡ Arrange meeting with Jo to agree what my current priorities really are (10/07).

➡ Arrange to see project accountant to understand what's important for me to focus on (03/07).

➡ Share my goal re food and drink with at least three other people and request support (05/04).

5 Date to complete or review the objective

Here we record the relevant dates for completion or review of the initial objective, e.g. 'Reduce my working day to eight hours.' It's often a good idea to put a review date in before the final date, in order to check progress. For example, if my goal is to reduce my working day to eight hours within a three-month period, a review point after a month would make sense.

Other ways to encourage ongoing learning

If a personal development plan is not appropriate/possible, there are a variety of other ways a coach might suggest for a coachee to continue learning, including:

➡ Book recommendations, titles, authors.

➡ Audiotape the coaching sessions and give the tapes to the coachee.

➡ Home study courses.

➡ Night school.

➡ Start a personal development group – a community of like-minded people.

➡ Attend courses.

➡ Listen to training tapes/CDs.

➡ Get a colleague or friend to help focus the coachee on their ongoing learning.

➡ Ask for regular feedback from friends or colleagues.

The list is probably much longer, and a coach is limited only by their imagination. I would suggest that the option be both pragmatic and desirable for the coachee. It's no good suggesting books to people who don't like reading, or night school to someone who has to look after small children in the evenings. Simple things work best, as they are most likely to happen. For someone with a regular drive to work, maybe tapes for the car are good, or for a long train journey a book might be a welcome distraction.

Make sure an individual feels supported

What's really great about a coaching relationship is the level of involvement and support that a good coach can create for the person they are working with. When that's gone, an individual may sometimes experience that as a sudden withdrawal of support. To avoid this happening, the coach needs to:

➡ Prepare the coachee for the session's ending.

➡ Identify other potential ways the coachee may get support if that's needed.

➡ Check back on the coachee shortly after the coaching has ended.

The preparation for the assignment to end will normally have happened long before the final coaching session. This begins by initially setting goals for the coaching assignment, reviewing progress, affirming learning, preparing for ongoing learning, etc. However when it is actually over, and the coach doesn't turn up the following month, some sense of withdrawal may still be felt. One simple option is for the coach to make one or two phone calls a little time after the coaching has ended. These don't have to be coaching conversations, although there is an obvious opportunity to offer a little reassurance, guidance or encouragement if needed.

Where the individual still wants and perhaps needs support, then the coach might consider other ways in which they might have that. Options of finding a 'buddy' or mentor can sometimes work, especially where the coaching has been done in a business environment. Where the sponsor of the coaching is actually the coachee's manager, perhaps they might be willing to meet with the coachee on a regular basis to discuss their performance or progress. This option has some advantages, in that the manager becomes more involved in what's happening with the individual who works for them. One disadvantage might be that the boss simply isn't the right person to listen to the coachee, maybe they're too busy, or perhaps the coachee doesn't feel able to discuss certain issues with them. Other alternatives within work might be a friend or colleague, someone in the training or personnel/HR department etc.

Checklist **Are we complete?**

At the closing stages of a coaching assignment, ask yourself the following questions to make sure the sessions are complete:

Q Have you had a conversation with the coachee to find out what they thought of the coaching?

Q Is the coachee comfortable that the coaching is coming to an end?

Q Does the coachee now have other goals or learning objectives, e.g. how they might improve even more at something?

Q Is the coachee clear about how their learning can be supported from now on, e.g. asking for regular feedback from colleagues, finding a mentor, etc.?

Q Are there any other stakeholders you need to update or complete the coaching process with, e.g. managers, training department, etc.?

A framework for coaching

Figure 4.2 illustrates our framework for a coaching assignment, and may be useful both as an initial overview and subsequent checklist.

Figure 4.2 summarizes the key activities described previously. These activities are intended to occur in most coaching assignments in some way. For example, whether an assignment is two sessions long or ten sessions long, it's still possible to have some form of review or confirmation of learning, etc.

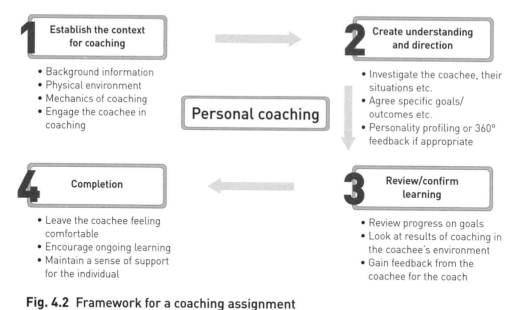

Fig. 4.2 Framework for a coaching assignment

Separate selling from coaching

You will notice that the activity of selling coaching services, agreeing fees and payment terms, etc. does not form part of the main coaching framework above. This is because selling coaching as a service would normally happen before any coaching session takes place. I would advise that, as much as possible, the coach endeavour to keep separate any conversations to negotiate fees or services from the actual coaching conversation. The coach and the coachee might struggle to concentrate on coaching goals and objectives if they have just been agreeing details relating to money or conditions of a contract.

When coaching in business, financial considerations rarely impinge on the coaching relationship. The individual enlisting the coach's services is often different from the person receiving them. For example, an HR or training manager might easily purchase coaching services for senior managers within the organization. Consequently, all matters of a financial nature will normally remain separate from the actual coaching sessions.

The order of coaching stages/activities

It makes sense to discuss the stages of coaching in the order that they logically arise. Using Fig. 4.2, this appears to be 1 Establish context, 2 Create understanding and direction, 3 Review /confirm learning and 4 Create closure.

My sequence of coaching stages is based on what seems to make sense, but it is not what always happens. After all, a coach might easily decide to establish ways that the coachee can obtain further support for their learning from the very first session. Whilst this normally is part of closure activity, it can also be valuable to promote from the outset.

Note too that one stage or activity does not necessarily equal one coaching session. For example, the initial coaching session will see the coach working on engaging the coachee's commitment, plus activities related to understanding the coachee and their current goals.

Checklist   How much structure do I need?

Questions that a coach might consider before deciding how much and when to use the coaching structure include:

Q What do I already know of the objectives for this coaching assignment?

Q How many coaching sessions will there be with this person?

Q Where will the coaching take place?

Q What is the total duration of the coaching assignment, e.g. three months?

Q Who is the true sponsor of this assignment – how should I involve them?

Q How long should/can each session last?

Q What experience of coaching or training might this person have had previously?

For example, if an individual has no experience of either coaching or training, I might choose to spend a little more time explaining coaching, or have them read an overview of coaching as preparation. Or, if they have had personal training or coaching before, I'd want to ask them about that. Then we could acknowledge any differences we might expect from the coaching approach I'm using.

Chapter summary Coaching process and structure

Any coaching assignment benefits from some advance preparation by the coach. For some assignments, that demands a fairly rigorous assessment of the nature of and objectives for the relationship. The coach may decide on formal checkpoints or reviews, use of 360° feedback, shadowing in the workplace etc. All of this must be planned for and organized.

For other assignments, it simply means thinking through some options, looking at the general nature of the situation and staying open and flexible as to how to progress the coaching sessions. In the end there's no right or wrong, only choices to be made. What's important is that a coach makes that choice in the knowledge of their options and the potential outcomes involved.

A coaching assignment can be highly enjoyable and fulfilling. By spending a little more time planning how you want your assignment to work, you can increase not only your enjoyment, but your effectiveness as well.

chapter

5

Fundamental skills
of coaching

There are some basic skills that can be learnt and developed that will distinguish a good coach from a 'not so good' coach. We all have some level of ability related to the skills, e.g. our existing ability to develop rapport. Other skills come less naturally, such as effective questioning, and may require learning and constant practice. I would recommend that anyone serious about a coaching profession take their own training very seriously. Untrained or sub-standard coaches can do more harm than good, creating an experience that's counterproductive for both the coach and the coachee.

Once skills are acquired, it's not like riding a bike – coaches do forget! These skills are more like muscles; they must be used regularly to keep them strong.

Can anyone coach?

In theory, anyone should be able to coach. In practice, however, some people are better suited to coaching than others. Perhaps because of their natural character traits, attitudes and basic motivations, some individuals find that coaching is a natural continuation of who they already are, and what they already do. Others find coaching conversations complicated, laborious, frustrating or even pointless. I would balance that by saying that if any individual were truly committed to developing the skills necessary to coach effectively, then that commitment would make it possible.

Fig. 5.1 Fundamental coaching skills

This chapter focuses on the fundamental skills of coaching, as illustrated in Fig. 5.1. Only within a coaching type of conversation are you likely to be focusing on so many skills all at once. Of course many routine activities contain several of the following skills, the most obvious being basic conversation! However, for someone to use the full set of skills in all conversations would be tiring for the individual and rather strange for those they were talking to.

Skill one – building rapport or relationship

Rapport – the dance behind communication

The foundation for all coaching conversations is a feeling of warmth and trust felt between the coach and the coachee. Great coaches are fabulous to talk to, and the coachee will experience them as warm, attentive and easy to relate to. This is due to the coach's ability to build rapport with other people. Many people outside the coaching profession have this skill. You can probably think of someone you know who is able to put people at their ease, and quickly build a feeling of familiarity or comfort when speaking to others.

Great coaches are fabulous to talk to.

Some people are able to do this naturally, while for others it is a skill they choose to develop. For a coach it is essential that they learn exactly how rapport happens, why it sometimes doesn't happen, and what options they have for building rapport. A coach needs to build more flexibility with the skill, in order to deal with the vast array of people they might meet in a coaching situation.

Let's look at rapport a little more closely. The word rapport describes the amount of warmth present in a conversation, and is affected by how 'related' or 'connected' the conversationalists feel. If you have good rapport with someone, you will normally feel more comfortable and relaxed in their company. I say 'normally' because that of course depends on what levels of rapport you want with the other person. Certain situations of close rapport may be undesirable to you. For example, if you meet someone you instantly feel attracted to, and you already have a partner!

An exercise Who do you have great rapport with?

Think of a friend or colleague with whom you believe you have great rapport. This will probably be someone with whom you have a good, easy-going relationship, someone who you feel comfortable talking with, someone whose company you enjoy. As you think about them, ask yourself:

Q How do I feel when I'm talking to them?

Q What does it feel like to be with them?

Q What similarities are there between me and this person?

You also probably know of someone who you simply can't seem to 'relate' to, even when you try. You might notice an increased sense of difference or separation between the two of you when conversing. You find easy, relaxed conversation more difficult, and perhaps there is even a sense of 'coldness' between you.

In this situation, you might easily argue that you have no rapport at all, since that's what it feels like. However, because rapport relates to the quality of relationship happening in the conversation, some sort of relatedness, albeit pretty negative, is still there. It's a little like discussing the quality of light in a room. Even when there appears to be no light, there still is some. Figure 5.2 illustrates how a scale of rapport might look.

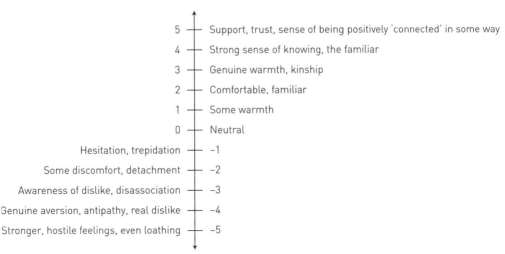

Fig. 5.2 Scale of rapport*

It is useful to remember that rapport is present in every form of conversation you ever have, at some level. This includes telephone conversations and even written conversations, as well as those that happen face to face. There might be a steamy kind of rapport in a conversation between lovers, a familiar warmth between old friends, or even an ice-cold relationship between two adversaries.

What creates rapport?

Where there is a high degree of 'sameness' between two individuals, we build rapport more easily. Perhaps instinctively we feel less threatened by someone we feel is like us, and more easily able to relax and open up to them. Categories of 'sameness' can include many different aspects, for example:

➡ Physical appearance/Clothes.

➡ Body language/Physical gestures.

➡ Qualities of voice.

➡ Language/Words used.

➡ Beliefs and values.

Let's look at each of these categories in more detail.

*Inspired by Genie Z. Laborde

Physical appearance/Clothes

For many of us, physical appearance has a huge effect on rapport. If we generally look similar, in colour, age, height, weight and features, we will tend to be more comfortable with each other. We might even say that two people 'look' like a couple, as an indication that they are well suited for a relationship or marriage.

If we dress in fairly similar ways, e.g. generally Western style, again, we have almost a subconscious tendency to feel we are alike. For example, if a Kalahari bushman walked in to Christmas luncheon wearing only a loincloth, and a few beads, feathers and face paint, they might have little natural rapport with the other guests there. Unless of course they were with the rest of their tribe in the Kalahari!

Body language/Physical gestures

Where two people are shown to have good rapport, they can often be seen as having similar or co-ordinating body language. If seated, they might adopt a similar pose; if one person leans forward, so might the other; if one rests on an elbow, the other might easily follow. It's easy to observe this yourself, simply by finding some people and watching them. Have a go at the exercise below for a little harmless fun.

An exercise **Go watch some rapport**

This is a nice, easy exercise. Go anywhere where there are couples, or groups of people. Spend some time watching them talk and interact. Notice the 'dance' between them, how they move together, away from each other, how they stand or position themselves in relationship to each other. Ask yourself the following questions:

Q How do you know whether people are enjoying each other's company by watching them?

Q How can you tell whether people are old friends or strangers?

Q What seems to be affecting the way people move or behave?

The more prominent signs of rapport are easy to notice. Postures, gestures, range of movement, the amount of energy they both have – you'll easily guess which conversational pairs have good rapport and which haven't.

Be careful to notice however some of the more subtle signs of rapport, as they can often lead to clues of something else going on. For example, imagine you're watching two different couples in a restaurant. The first couple is animated in their conversation, both giving each other lots of eye contact, using similar gestures and poses. You'd easily guess that this couple has high levels of rapport and comfort with each other.

You then notice a second couple, sitting much more quietly, not talking very much, not looking at each other very much, moving with much less energy and animation. You might decide that this couple has a low level of rapport, as you interpret their lack of conversation and energy to mean 'coldness'. Surprisingly, you then see one of them rest a hand lovingly on their partner's and a momentary gaze of real affection pass between them. Then, as if nothing had passed between them, they return to their meal.

One explanation might be as follows. The first couple is in the first flushes of romance and just getting to know each other. Their energy and animation comes from the excitement and anticipation of such a new relationship. Other signs of their rapport include matching facial expressions, movements toward each other – this is a dance of courtship.

The second couple has been very happily married for many years, they are completely at ease and are simply a little tired that evening. Signs of their comfort, relationship and love for each other are again reflected in the similarities of their behaviour. There are signs of a dance; it's simply more of a slow waltz than a samba.

I would also guess that this second couple has a much deeper level of rapport and relatedness than the first, based on a real sense of connection and intimacy.

Qualities of voice

The way voices sound can also give a real indication of rapport within a conversation. I'm referring to our tone of voice, speed of speech and timbre (deep voice, high-pitched, etc.). We convey a tremendous amount of meaning with these voice qualities, as the quick exercise below demonstrates:

An exercise Change your meaning and not your words

Using the phrase 'Yes all right then', repeat it three different times, changing
the quality of your voice each time, using the following characteristics:

➡ Bored and slightly irritated.

➡ Trying to hide your excitement.

➡ Resigned but compliant.

Notice how the meaning or intention of the phrase changes each time your voice quality
changes.

Like physical postures, the balance of your voice qualities can also illustrate your rapport
with someone. Where two people in conversation have great rapport, there will be a
matching of some of their voice qualities. The amount of
energy in their speech, perhaps the speed at which they are
talking, might all be similar.

**Where key qualities of
voice are not matched, you
might notice a lack of
rapport.**

Where key qualities of voice are not matched, you might
notice a lack of rapport. One common mistake people make is
to speak slowly and calmly to someone who's very angry, hoping it might calm them
down. Sometimes it simply makes them worse. Imagine you've stayed at home for the
third day running for someone to come and fix your TV set, and again the repair van has
not arrived. After 20 minutes, you finally get through the repair company's telephone
system to the operator. By now you're feeling pretty angry. You begin to explain the situation (angrily!), only to be greeted by slow, deep, warm tones cooing 'All right . . . I'm
just going to need a few more details from you . . . then [soothingly] we can get this
whole thing sorted for you.'

As a caller, you're quite likely to feel patronized, and as though your complaint isn't being
taken seriously enough. After all you're the only one who seems to feel upset by it!

The problem lies in the mismatch of voices. The operator would get a better result if she
matched your speed of speech and character of voice. By speaking more like you, she

could begin to build a sense of understanding and relatedness between you. For example (spoken quickly, with strength and purpose), 'Right, I'm going to need a few more details – I want to sort this out for you quickly now.'

As a caller, you will then believe your problem has a sense of significance, simply because the operator is speaking with similar voice qualities to you. In turn, this probably has a calming effect, and your own speech may become gentler. If the operator is skilled, she'll continue matching you, and her own voice will also become 'calmer'.

An exercise **Change your voice**

Find someone who speaks in one of these ways:

➡ Much more slowly than you.

➡ Much more loudly or quietly than you.

➡ In a much lower or higher pitched voice.

If you want a 'stretch', you can also do it with someone who speaks much more quickly than you do, but be warned, it can be a challenge to keep up!

The first time you do this, I'd recommend you tell the other person what you're doing. That way you can find out how it felt for them, how comfortable they felt, etc. When you think you've mastered the technique, use it whenever it seems appropriate for rapport.

Step one

Have a conversation with them, about something they are interested in, perhaps a hobby or particular area of study or learning. As the conversation progresses, gradually match their pace of speaking a little more closely. If they speak more slowly, gradually slow down your speech; if they are quiet, speak more quietly. Notice how your focus or attention has to change in order for you to do this. Do this as naturally as possible. Often slight adjustments work better than becoming an exact match of the other person.

Step two

Afterwards, consider the following questions:

Q What did you have to focus on to be able to do this?

Q What effect did your 'matching' seem to have (on you and on the other person)?

Q How did this affect the amount of rapport you felt?

If possible, ask the same questions of the person you were talking to. That way you'll get even more learning from the exercise.

Language/Words used

We tend to notice the importance of words for rapport only when we get it wrong! For example, here is the initial part of a coaching conversation:

COACH:	'So, Jim, it's been nearly a month hasn't it? How have you been?'
JIM:	'Well, okay I guess, I've kinda been feeling a little low though, a bit under the weather as they say.'
COACH:	'Sorry to hear that – how long have you been depressed then?'
JIM:	'Oh I'm not depressed! I just said a little low – how do you get from that I'm depressed?'

As coach, you're now into a bit of a recovery situation, early on in your conversation – not a great start! This could have been avoided by repeating the same key words the coachee used.

As a more positive example, have you noticed how groups or communities of people often adopt the same words or phrases as each other? We notice this within certain professions or occupations especially. For example:

Phrase	Meaning
'That's a wrap'	'We're finished/we're done here'
'Let's take that off-line'	'Let's discuss outside of this group we're in now'
'You're a star'	'You're great/thanks/well done'
'Break a leg'	'I hope it goes well for you'
'Same old same old'	'Nothing changes'

Whether you're in construction, finance, the theatre, or any other profession, you're likely to have your own words or phrases that help you feel related as a community. If you find yourself on the 'outside' of this kind of language, i.e. you don't understand it and can't use it, it's possible to feel alienated quite quickly.

An exercise Who's playing word games?

Over the next few days, observe other people talking together in your work or social life (or simply go somewhere else and eavesdrop!). Listen to conversations, in particular the actual words and catchy phrases that are being used. Judge for yourself the amount of rapport between people. Then consider:

Q What types of buzzwords or phrases are being used?

Q How much are these words being copied or repeated by individuals?

Q What effect is this copying having on the conversation?

Let's look at the previous coaching dialogue now – with the coach more careful this time to match the individual's words:

COACH: 'So, Jim, it's been nearly a month hasn't it? How have you been?'

JIM: 'Well, okay I guess, I've kinda been feeling a little low though, a bit under the weather as they say.'

COACH: 'You've been feeling a little low?'

JIM: 'Yeah, you know, just odd days, its almost like there's a little grey cloud over my head and it won't be shifted.'

COACH: 'This cloud – what's it about, what's in it?'

You'll notice that the coach not only matches the words the coachee is using, but also the 'sense' of the images the coachee is building, e.g. by asking what's 'in' the cloud. As the coachee begins to feel understood, he begins to relax and explain what he's been feeling.

Coach's corner Watch my feelings

Where we want to acknowledge feelings

Sometimes, we need to acknowledge someone's feelings as a way of empathizing with them, or demonstrating an understanding of what they've said. Here, it usually works best to use the exact words or phrase they use. This is especially true when those feelings are negative. For example, if they say they're upset, say 'I appreciate that you're upset.' If they say they're worn out, use the words 'worn out' (not 'fatigued' or 'dog-tired').

Where we want to influence feelings

Sometimes, you might want to reduce the significance of someone's feelings in the conversation. Maybe you wish to make them feel a little better about what they felt, or help them calm down a little. If you have good rapport, use a diluted or reduced version of their word. For example, they say 'I'm scared stiff of making presentations' and you don't want to keep them thinking about that. When you refer to these feelings, you might substitute for 'scared stiff', 'apprehensive' or 'uncomfortable', e.g. 'I guess you'd want to let go of some of those feelings of apprehension wouldn't you?' You can then begin to use more positive imagery and feelings, e.g. 'What would it take for you to feel fantastic about giving a presentation?'

Beliefs and values

What we believe to be true about our world and ourselves can either separate or bring people together. Religion is an obvious example of how beliefs can separate or unite people. On a simpler note, watch a passionate meat eater debate with a vegan about their eating habits and you'll see and hear how beliefs can divide.

Notice how a salesperson might find common ground with a potential client, to increase their ability to enrol that client. A good salesman will often spend time learning about their client as a person, what they do, what they like, and what they don't like. By agreeing with the client on topics that they appear passionate about, e.g. the importance of a good education (or even the irrelevance of one), they build rapport based on implied like-mindedness. We tend to buy products and services from people we 'like', and we have a related tendency to like people who we believe are 'like' us. Building rapport is obviously a key behaviour for people in sales professions.

When to increase rapport

As well as knowing the factors involved in developing rapport, we should also know **when** to work at improving it. Sometimes, this simply isn't necessary. By working to increase rapport when there is no need, you divert your attention from other key aspects, such as listening. Additionally, you may alter your behaviour to the point where you begin to mismatch and that will actually make things worse!

Where the coachee appears comfortable with the conversation, looks and sounds fairly relaxed, and is showing no signs of alienation or disassociation, my tendency is usually to forget about building rapport.

One point where I often work to enhance rapport in coaching conversations comes during the initial stages of the assignment. At this point, any individual I'm working with may need to feel more comfortable with me before they begin to trust me, and open up to the process of coaching.

The other obvious place where I must make sure I am building good rapport is at the start of each coaching conversation. No matter how warm or open our previous conversations, the time and distance between sessions creates the need to re-affirm the coaching relationship.

Increasing rapport through simple matching

One well-known way of increasing rapport is known as matching. This means being literally the same in some way as the person you want to build rapport with. Within a coaching environment, simple ways of building rapport would include matching posture, voice quality, speed of speech, physical gestures etc.

When I'm coaching, and decide that rapport isn't as good as I need it to be, I'll first look for mismatches or differences between us. I'll do a quick check on physical posture, voice qualities, amounts of energy we're displaying – obvious things that I can easily adapt. If my gestures are more animated than the other person's, I'll calm myself down a little. If I'm speaking much more quickly than they are, I'll begin to decrease my pace. Do this as a gradual process, so that the other person does not consciously notice it.

Most often, I'll begin by subtly matching physical posture, as that has multiple benefits. First, it helps me to begin to focus more on the individual, think more about what's happening with them, and less about what's happening with me. Secondly, it does often improve rapport quite rapidly. Thirdly – and perhaps 'weirdly' – once I begin to attune to the individual in this way, my concentration seems to increase or shifts, so that at some level I begin to notice other behaviours exhibited by the other person. These might include subtle facial expressions, eye movements, changes in skin tone, etc. Often I am able to 'pick up' or 'read' other signals that previously I might have been missing.

When is matching actually mismatching?

A word of caution on simple matching. If you 'overdo it', that is, match someone very obviously, or to an extreme level of detail, then instead of building rapport you will actually alienate the individual. There's nothing worse than having someone 'mirror' your every movement, behaviour and gesture. When you lift your hand – they lift their hand, when you cough – they cough. Sooner or later, you'll notice that you have what appears to be a very strange person behaving oddly in front of you! Instead of helping you feel more comfortable, you'll feel exactly the opposite.

Matching effectively is a subtle art. If you want to match someone who is leaning forward, first incline your body slightly towards them. If someone is continually smoothing their eyebrow, brush your hand across your own. If they continually clasp or wring their hands, then occasionally bring yours together. I know this might sound strange but it works!

The question of eye contact

Some people try to increase rapport with another person by looking directly into their eyes, for long periods of time. You might find that people in retail or sales professions are actually trained to do this when talking to customers. This is by no means guaranteed to improve the customer's sense of comfort with them, especially if the individual adds the trick of not blinking! Many people do not like to be 'stared' or 'gazed' at, and some may even find it threatening.

It is also possible that some people relate sustained, direct eye contact with memories of being disciplined or reprimanded in childhood. Sadly, parents often spend most time looking into their children's eyes when they are telling them how naughty or bad they've been. This might explain why some children grow up into adults who don't enjoy lots of eye contact with others.

Again, when judging how much eye contact is appropriate with another person, we should work at matching them.

If the other person appears to give you lots of eye contact, then they'll be comfortable with you doing the same. If they look at you less frequently, then they are likely to respond to a similar level of eye contact. Simply notice and match the approximate proportions of time spent looking directly at the other person.

When to decrease rapport

There are times when it is entirely appropriate to decrease rapport or the levels of relationship that are occurring during the conversation. For example, when you want to close a conversation down, draw an end to the session and begin to summarize the key points and agree on actions.

There are also appropriate levels of rapport for the coaching relationship, and inappropriate levels. Should too much familiarity, intimacy or warmth occur between the coach

There are also appropriate levels of rapport for the coaching relationship, and inappropriate levels.

and the coachee, it is very easy for the relationship to become one of friendship, rather than a purposeful arrangement between two people.

For years, I found it incredibly difficult to coach my friends, and impossible to coach my family and this is one reason why! Other reasons relate to emotional attachment and personal agenda, which we'll cover later in the book.

When deciding to decrease rapport, the same principles apply as for increasing rapport, although often in reverse. For example, you may be talking to someone and want to end the discussion in order to get to your next meeting. The person you're talking to is obviously unaware that you want to close the conversation down. Simply notice where you are directly matching the other person, and then gradually begin to mismatch. Change your posture so that you're different. If their voice qualities are both warm and steady, put a little more energy back into yours.

Again, adopt these new behaviours gradually, or the individual may notice the stark contrast in what you're doing. If you've had good rapport, you may notice that they begin to match you, e.g. sit up straighter, begin to nod, etc. That's OK, as they will also begin to notice signs of a closing conversation. Where you have done this subtly, and have had previously good rapport, this will normally be experienced as a polite gesture.

An exercise   Increasing and decreasing rapport

This is a very simple, basic technique for demonstrating our ability to both increase and decrease rapport. It works by increasing or reducing a physical sense of 'sameness'. To do it, you'll first need a willing partner, and somewhere quiet to sit where you won't be interrupted.

Tell your partner you want to do an exercise in rapport, but don't go into any detail. Ask them to talk about something they can discuss easily, e.g. a favourite holiday or pastime.

Step one – talk and observe

Begin the conversation. Ask your partner questions, get them talking. Notice their physical posture and gestures as they speak.

Step two – increase rapport by matching

Continue talking to them, and begin to subtly match their posture and gestures. If they're leaning forward, lean in, if moving a lot, increase your own movement. Continue doing this until you are comfortable that you're matching well. Do it for a couple of minutes.

Step three – decrease rapport by mismatching

Continue talking, and begin to deliberately mismatch what they're doing. Fold your arms, look away, cross your legs – be really different! Do this until you're sure it's had an effect – or until you can't carry on for laughing. (It's not easy and they'll know you're doing it!)

Step four – talk about what happened

Explain to your partner the three-step process, then ask them:

Q   Did they notice when you started matching them?

Q   What effect did matching them have?

Q   What effect did mismatching them have?

The optional 'stretch'

If you find the exercise seems too easy, then match and mismatch on any (or all) of the following:

➡ Their breathing.

➡ Their voice qualities – pitch, pace, tone etc.

➡ The key words or phrases they seem to use.

The importance of intention

Our intention within a conversation with someone can have a dramatic impact on the sense of relatedness we might have with that person. You might experience intention as a sense of purpose, or perhaps an aim for the conversation. Shifting our intention changes our focus. This can be useful where we've tried some simple matching and rapport still isn't as good as we want it. For example, you may begin to wonder how else you might be alike, in order to increase the rapport between you and the other person. You can do this by focusing on a simple thought such as 'How else are we related or alike?'

In a coaching conversation, this may provoke thoughts of common beliefs you've previously shared, or ways in which you are basically related. For example, you might have several shared goals. You might remember that you both want the conversation to be productive and effective, and you both want to surface information or insights that will cause the conversation to be worthwhile. It is always possible to find some way in which you are related to another person, even if that's simply in your humanness.

In my own experience, this often allows me to deepen the levels of rapport between the other person and myself. Sometimes this is because it was me who was blocking rapport, and all I've done is remove my own thoughts of separation or difference.

None of my internal thoughts or questions is communicated verbally to the person I'm coaching. At this point, I'm simply using the power of my own intention to focus my own mind to where I want it to go. I'm using short, straightforward questions as thoughts as I concentrate on increasing my sense of relatedness to the other person. Before you think I've gone completely mad, let me explain a little more.

By the term 'power of intention', I refer to our innate ability to direct or concentrate our thoughts in order to create a specific outcome. In this instance we're using the intention of deepening rapport, coupled with a question, or thought, such as 'How can I increase my relatedness to him/her?'

Gradually, as I leave the question suspended in my thoughts, I begin to understand how. Maybe I'll suddenly realize that I'm staring too intently and this might be disconcerting, maybe I'm talking too much, or not enough.

An exercise Use your intention

When we focus our minds on our intention, our thoughts and behaviours can often marshal themselves to show us the appropriate way forward. So go and have a conversation with someone you know quite well, but not very well. If you can choose someone who you'd like better rapport with then that might work even better.

During the conversation, have an intention to have great rapport with the other person. You want to develop that warmth and sense of connection that comes from having great rapport. You might use a word or phrase to remind yourself occasionally of this intention, for example: 'warmth and openness' or 'relationship'. During the conversation, simply remember the thought or phrase as much as seems appropriate. Remember that you also want to be able to have a conversation, so only concentrate on the thought as much as seems comfortable. If the thought begins to act as a distraction, then forget it – let it go.

After the conversation, ask yourself:

Q What was the rapport like within the conversation?

Q How did using your intention appear to affect your rapport?

Q How could you use your intention in the future?

Developing the coaching relationship over time

As a coach, once you've established rapport, you will then develop that relationship throughout your involvement with the coachee. The duration of your relationship might be just one coaching session, or it could last many months or even years. In many coaching assignments an ongoing relationship is needed. So we need to consider the factors that will affect the sense of mutual warmth and value over a period of time. The following adds to the previous aspects of rapport, to give us a fuller appreciation of the importance of developing a coaching relationship over time.

Integrity

Integrity refers to the alignment between what we know to be true, right, wrong, good, bad and what we actually do. For example, if you know it's wrong to steal, then don't steal. If you believe it's wrong to lie, then don't lie. Integrity is a black and white, simple principle. For all that, integrity is not something that comes easily to many of us. For example, stealing logically covers all forms of theft, from stealing folding money to not putting a ticket on our car in the car park. When we're pressured, short on time, or not feeling abundant, how easy is it to decide not to do what we say is 'right'? In the example of lying, are so-called 'white' lies still lies? – Yes they are! So integrity calls upon us to be incredibly powerful in our own behaviours. To act consistently from a sense of personal integrity involves a lifetime of learning for most of us. Fortunately, in coaching the examples are probably simpler to debate and easier to adopt as personal standards.

As a coach, what we say must match what we do.

Integrity causes us to be of our word. As a coach, what we say must match what we do. If you say you're going to call your coachee, then call them. If you say you're going to post them some information on Friday then post it on Friday. This simple congruence of words and actions is very powerful within a coaching relationship. Your coachee is more likely to trust and respect you when you keep your commitments to them. This forms a contribution from you to the coachee, and over time your relationship will benefit. In addition, this can have a positive influence on a coachee's own behaviours. By setting high standards of personal behaviour you personally demonstrate to the coachee what works and what doesn't. The consistency of your behaviours forms a further support to the coaching conversations.

Where a coach does not keep a commitment, they need to do whatever is appropriate to redress the situation. For example, if they didn't send information as promised, it's probably appropriate to apologize, and offer to send on the information if it is still needed. If the coach didn't call, then the coach can acknowledge that, e.g. apologize, and do whatever is needed to meet the needs of the call that didn't happen. If it helps the situation, then sometimes it's appropriate to explain why a commitment hasn't been kept. Maybe you're late because your car broke down. I'm cautious about over-explaining these reasons, as our explanations can easily become excuses. These excuses enable us to avoid responsibility for our actions. For example, we sometimes use the excuse of heavy traffic for being late. Actually, we're late because we just didn't leave the house early enough!

From personal experience, I find the best way to keep my commitments is to:

➡ Make commitments wisely – Can I keep this commitment? Is this a good/reasonable commitment to make?

➡ Make commitments important, record them, make them a priority task

➡ Deal with the consequences of any commitments I haven't kept, e.g. apologize, make amends if possible (doing this encourages you to simply keep them in the first place!).

So if you're doubtful about whether or not you can keep a commitment don't make it! Or simply make an adapted version of the commitment, e.g. 'I'll post you the information on Friday if I get some free time, otherwise it will be either Monday or Tuesday of next week'. By building in an extension to the deadline, we increase our chances of meeting the commitment.

An exercise   Are you keeping commitments?

Use the following questions to reflect on your current tendency to keep commitments or promises made. If you're not able to answer them immediately, then use them to monitor your behaviour over the next few days, or even weeks.

Q   How readily do you make commitments or promises to do things, e.g. hear yourself saying 'I'll do that/send that by . . .' or 'I'll call you'? This includes doing things for yourself, e.g. 'I'm going to book that appointment this week.'

Q   How many of your promises or commitments do you actually keep exactly as voiced, e.g. by the deadline you gave?

Q   If you don't keep a commitment what do you do, e.g. ignore the fact, use excuses to avoid responsibility or simply put it right?

When you have some answers to the above, consider the following question:

Q   Which of the following could you use to get even better at dealing with your commitments?

➡ Make commitments wisely – Can I keep this commitment? Is this a good/reasonable commitment to make?

➡ Make commitments important, record them, make them a priority task.

➡ Deal with the consequences of any commitments not kept, e.g. apologize, make amends if possible.

Openness and trust

A really successful coaching relationship will include a sense of openness and trust between the coach and the coachee. The coach can encourage this by being open with the coachee and being someone whom they can trust. The following are all ways that a coach can promote this trust and openness:

➡ Share personal facts and details occasionally, e.g. mention your family circumstances, discuss personal plans, goals etc.

➡ Declare own thoughts and feelings sometimes, e.g. about events outside of coaching.

➡ Speak your own truth consistently (see Strategizing in the conversation p. 207)

➡ Be of your word (keep commitments made).

➡ Keep any confidences between you and the coachee.

➡ Support the coachee in conversation outside of the coaching sessions, e.g. don't say anything about the coachee that you wouldn't want them to hear afterwards.

➡ Act in the coachee's best interests at all times, e.g. stay focused on their goals, make their success and fulfilment a priority during your conversations with them.

Section summary — Building rapport or relationship

As a coaching skill, the ability to influence levels of rapport during conversations enables a coach to gain both trust, buy-in and influence within the coaching conversations. Good rapport refers to the quality of relationship happening in the conversation, as the conversation is happening. It is directly affected by our thoughts or feelings being in some way the same or different to the other person. Where we are alike, we like, but where we are different, we don't like! Traditional techniques of simple physical matching do have a level of influence. However, other factors may be much more important. Our sense of shared values, common aims and intentions can be the underlying factors that create real relatedness within the conversation.

Over time, the positive development of a coaching relationship is affected by principles such as integrity, consistency, openness and trust. Our ability to act consistently from these principles influences both the coaching relationship and the coachee's own behaviour. The demands on the coach for high standards of personal behaviour require both commitment and self-discipline. The rewards of great coaching relationships and a clear conscience are worth the effort!

Skill two – different levels of listening

The art of listening is generally misunderstood and underrated as a skill – I firmly believe we should teach it in schools! The potential benefits of listening, for both the listener and the speaker, are not often acknowledged or valued. For example, good listeners obtain better understanding of people and situations. Someone who has that better understanding can respond to situations more effectively than someone who hasn't. Simple instances such as following travel directions, taking down telephone messages etc. are everyday occurrences that challenge our ability to listen.

In business, I notice good listeners make fewer mistakes, upset fewer people, and generally operate using better quality information. Good listeners also make a contribution to the person speaking. The person speaking benefits by being encouraged to share their thoughts and ideas, viewed as someone who has valid opinions.

For our community as a whole, if we raised the average quality of our listening for each other, we'd see greater mutual understanding, increase the generation of new ideas, experience fewer disputes, and probably avoid a few small wars!

Much of the time, the consequences of poor listening aren't desperate, they're simply frustrating. Maybe we missed an appointment, maybe we didn't appreciate the full facts about something, or we missed an opportunity.

Sometimes, the consequences of poor listening are more important. Within coaching especially, poor listening by the coach can lead to an inability to understand a coachee and their situations. Where the coach is unable to develop this understanding, this becomes a real barrier to coaching.

The gift of listening

People who are great at listening can be found everywhere. Maybe you know someone you would call a 'good listener' or maybe you've had people say it about you. It is a compliment, because people like to be listened to. In fact, people love to be listened to! Sometimes, when someone listens to you, cares about what you say, and how you say it, explores your thoughts further, seeks to understand you – it can be like basking in sunlight. When we experience this kind of listening, we are able to open up, as we feel valued and acknowledged. It's almost as though we grow larger in the conversation, simply because of the quality of the other person's listening.

We have a saying 'a problem shared is a problem halved' that relates to the beneficial effects on a person when they and their problems are listened to. Somehow, in the telling and the listening, a problem shared diminishes in size or significance for its owner.

In this way, listening is a gift we can give others. It's a gift because it requires effort on the part of the listener, who must put aside their own self for a while, and focus entirely on someone else. When you've had a hard day, have complaints yourself, stories to tell, think about what it takes to put those to one side and listen attentively to someone else's day!

Most people don't find this easy. For a coach, no matter what's been happening before the coaching session, they must put personal events to one side and focus entirely on the person they are coaching.

Listening in order to influence

Strangely, people trying to influence, convince or 'sell' to others, often do more talking than listening. When we do most of the talking, we diminish our ability to draw information from other people. We reduce the space and time available to process information and so respond to it. People in sales professions will sometimes miss loud signals that the person will now buy from them, simply because they are in a 'talking' mode not a 'listening' one!

More regularly, people will pursue a line of debate or argument that's having no impact on the other person. If they switched instead to a mode of listening more, reflecting more on what the other person was saying, or doing, they might easily gain information that would help.

For example, imagine you want to get a reluctant friend or partner to book a holiday. You might spend a long time describing the location, the facilities, and weather conditions before realizing your own reasons for wanting the holiday might not be theirs! By spending more time listening to what their objections to the holiday really are, and what they really want, you are in a much better position to influence their thinking. Or simpler, to accept that there's no way they'll ever book the holiday and you're wasting your energy trying to persuade them!

Listening within coaching

All good coaches normally listen more closely and effectively than the average listener. A really good coach will have an ability to listen that often goes beyond the point at which most people are actually able to listen. As a result of their listening, a coach is able to pass beyond what is actually said, and begin to notice what is 'unsaid'.

For example, a coachee might be explaining how they are very excited about a forthcoming job move, describing how it's good for them right now to be moving in a certain direction, and how it feels 'right'. In their listening, the coach might actually hear something else that's not spoken, that completely contradicts what the coachee is saying. Perhaps the coach hears a change in the person's tone of voice, or something about their words that doesn't quite 'ring true'. This might be something very subtle that would be easily missed by poor listening.

By noticing this, the coach is able to make this observation, and potentially surface some reservations or anxieties about the job move. If a coach is able to deal both with what's spoken and unspoken, the conversation has much more depth for both speaker and listener.

What do we mean by levels of listening?

Our listening changes with the amount of focused effort we direct towards what (or who) we're listening to.

There are actually several different forms of listening, although generally we discuss the topic as though there were only one. We ask, 'Are you listening?' And we expect the answer to be 'Yes' or 'No', as if there's a listening switch that we can turn on or off. Perhaps a more accurate response would be 'Sort of . . .' or 'Just to the words' or 'All the way to behind what you were actually saying!' Our listening changes with the amount of focused effort we direct towards what (or who) we're listening to. After all, if you're only 'half listening' doesn't that take a lot less directed effort than 'listening intently'?

Figure 5.3 shows different forms of listening as though they were actually levels.

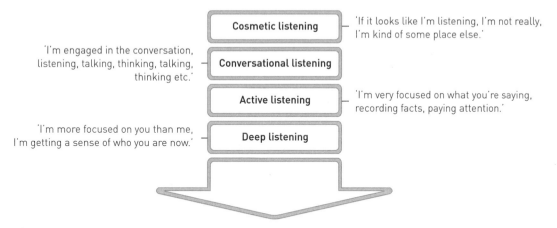

Figure 5.3 Levels of listening

As our level of listening deepens, so does our focus and attention on the person we are listening to. Let's look in more detail now at some of the ways that we listen to people.

Cosmetic listening

This you would probably recognize as 'pretending to listen'. That is, you're looking at someone, you might be nodding, and adding 'listening noises' such as 'Hmmm' or 'Yes' or 'That's interesting'. The person speaking may or may not be aware of the way you are listening to them, and may well be continuing to speak regardless.

What's also happening is that as the listener, most of your attention and thoughts are actually elsewhere. You might be thinking about something completely separate from what the other person is talking about, or considering thoughts or experiences thrown up by what's being said.

Occasionally, you might 'miss' something that the person has said, and realize you're losing track of the conversation, saying something like 'Sorry, I drifted off just then – what did you just say?'

Circumstances and your objectives for a conversation will indicate whether you are using an appropriate level of listening. For example, when listening to a child chatter, telling stories or reliving other conversations they've had with other children, this sort of listening is sometimes OK, and works for both you and the child. I would add the proviso, however, that sometimes it's great to really listen to children telling their stories, and can be like stepping into a whole other world! It's also a great way to demonstrate your care for a child, because by listening to them properly, they will feel valued by you, and that's good for building their self-esteem. And if that makes you feel like a better parent, then it's probably good for yours too!

Cosmetic listening may also be appropriate when you sense that the other person isn't actually talking to you – they're just enjoying talking, letting off steam perhaps, and require little input from you. It's probably wise to check back in to the conversation occasionally though, just in case you were missed!

This type of listening does not work in coaching, as your objectives for the conversation rely on you gathering information from the other person. I would acknowledge, however, that most coaches occasionally drift off into their own thoughts from time to time, and it's difficult to avoid. If it happens to a coach, and they miss a key point of information, I would recommend they be as open as possible, e.g. 'I'm sorry, whilst you were saying that, I was still thinking about your ideas for the new job – can you repeat that last thought?'

By declaring that you stopped fully listening, you re-affirm your commitment to listen, that is, the person speaking knows that what they say is still important to you. Also, most people would acknowledge that they sometimes do the same thing.

Conversational listening

This is the kind of listening that we do most of the time. In general conversation with others, we listen, talk, think, listen, think, talk and so on. Our focus is on the other person, what they're saying and also on what we're saying, thinking of saying, etc. The balance between talking, listening and internally processing information varies from person to person. This balance relates to several factors, including our basic personality type, the nature of the conversation, how we're feeling etc. Some people talk much more than they listen, some people prefer to speak less, listen more, and some appear to have a pretty even balance of both.

Again, your objectives for the conversation will affect your listening. A police officer gathering facts at the scene of a road traffic accident is more likely to listen and internally process information before asking further questions or making observations. A person teaching a specialized subject in a classroom situation is more likely to be doing more of the talking, and much less listening, or processing of information from the class.

Conversational listening is a natural activity for most people. It requires little effort, and is present in most of our normal, daily conversations, and it can be tremendous fun and really quite energizing.

Coaching conversations are not the same as these day-to-day conversations, however, simply because of their purpose. Within coaching, we must develop a deeper form of listening.

An exercise **Listen and learn**

Use your normal conversations today to consider the following:

Q How often do you pretend to listen to someone – and don't really listen?

Q How is your listening different, i.e. within different circumstances, or with different people?

Q What effect does the quality of your listening seem to have on other people or the conversation?

Active listening

One of the skills of listening a coach must have before they begin coaching is active listening, it has certain characteristics:

➡ The listener is using more effort to listen and process information than speaking themselves.

➡ The listener has the intention of staying focused on what the other person is saying, in order to fully understand what they are saying.

➡ The listener is mentally registering and recording facts so they can potentially use them later (they may even take notes).

➡ The listener continually confirms that they are still listening, by making appropriate sounds, gestures or expressions.

➡ The listener will actively seek to understand what the person is telling them, by using clarifying questions, repeating information back to them, offering observations or conclusions.

A conversation where the coach listens attentively might sound like this:

SPEAKER: 'So the whole interview turned into a bit of a nightmare. I ended up wondering why the heck they'd invited me in the first place.'

LISTENER: 'Really – why, what happened?'

SPEAKER: 'Well, firstly, they kept me sat in reception for ages, so it was three o'clock in the afternoon before I got into the interview. My appointment was for two.'

LISTENER: 'An hour late?'

SPEAKER: 'Exactly, anyway, then I got in and I'm greeted by the someone from Sales, and some bloke from the computer department – which was kind of strange. The least they could have done would have been to have someone in there relevant to the position they were hiring.'

LISTENER: 'What was the position?'

SPEAKER: 'Warehouse foreman – not the sort of job that you'd think those two would be interested in. They immediately started asking me about what type of warehouse operations I'd run in the past, and how much I'd used computers! Then the Sales guy starts getting interested in how the shops used to let us know what to order and what to deliver – they just kept going off at tangents.'

LISTENER: 'Right – so what did you do in the interview?'

SPEAKER: 'Well I just kept trying to bring them back to the important stuff like how important security is, and how to stop staff stealing things.'

LISTENER: 'Hmm – so what's happened since?'

SPEAKER: 'Nothing, not a thing, no letter, no phone call – nothing!'

You will notice from the dialogue that the listener is focusing very much on understanding what's happened. The listener is gathering facts, filling in gaps, working to get a fuller picture of events. The listener is not spending large amounts of energy giving their own thoughts and views, not telling stories of interviews that they've had, and not offering advice and ideas. These behaviours would fit more into the scope of 'conversational listening' described earlier.

The listener is also following a fairly logical time sequence, i.e. asking about actions or events in the order they would have happened. For example, the question 'What's happened since?' comes at the end of the conversation not the beginning. This enables the speaker to recollect information in a way that feels more natural to them.

Deep listening

This last category of listening is unlike any other, in that it goes beyond what it is logically possible to achieve by listening to someone. I have heard people describe good coaches as 'almost telepathic' because of their ability to listen to and understand another person, form insights into what they have said, or even understand what they have *not* said. These understandings and insights become possible when a coach is in a state of deep listening.

I have heard people describe good coaches as 'almost telepathic'.

When a coach is able to generate this quality of listening, they are able to experience the other person with a sense of who they are, as well as what they're saying. I can only describe this state of listening as a slightly altered mental state and would describe its characteristics as follows:

➡ The mind of the listener is mostly quiet and calm.

➡ The awareness of the listener is entirely focused on the other person.

➡ The listener has little or no sense or awareness of themselves.

➡ The listener is totally lucid and present to the person speaking.

➡ This state can easily be broken or disturbed, e.g. by the speaker asking the listener a question, or seeking acknowledgement of some sort.

This state of listening feels almost elusive in nature, in that once you realize you have it, are in it, the thought registers and it's gone again! This seemingly 'higher' state of listening has similar characteristics to meditation, in that the listener's mind is essentially quiet, with occasional thoughts or insights passing through.

Seeking to serve

What also seems present, however, is an intention towards the person you are listening to. In my experience, this intention is usually one of service – perhaps seeking to understand, seeking to help or provide support, something that contributes towards the individual and their learning.

For the listener, it almost feels as though you are experiencing 'being' the other person – although of course you are not. In terms of your ability to relate to the other person, what they are thinking and feeling about a situation, the quality of the information you are receiving is significant. For the person being listened to, as they are speaking they will undoubtedly feel understood, and they also might experience a deeper sense of relatedness to the listener.

I should add at this point that to stay in continual deep listening for extended periods of time is neither desirable nor possible. It is not possible because the coach cannot only listen, they must also make observations, question and generally stay in the conversation. Plus, like meditation, it's a real challenge to maintain such a quiet state of mind. Long periods of deep listening are not desirable, because the coaching process demands that you are more than a passive observer. As a coach you engage in dialogue, in order to facilitate the other person's thinking. Your speaking, questioning, physical gestures or expressions are all key to this process.

In addition, other forms of listening are sometimes more useful, for example, when you need to gather the facts of a situation first, or help someone 'get something off their chest'. In such cases attentive listening works a lot better, and more quickly.

Developing deep listening

I would recommend that anyone seriously committed to the field of coaching actively develop their own ability to listen in this way. Deep listening challenges us in a different way from a lot of other activities, possibly because working harder can actually work against us. The following exercise will help you develop your skill further.

An exercise Developing deep listening

What is this? ➡ An exercise for listening to someone that creates a deeper understanding of them and their thoughts.

How would I use it? ➡ You'll need someone to do this with you, who knows what you're doing, and why. That way you can ask them for feedback and you'll learn faster. Once you're comfortable with the style of listening, you can use it anywhere you like. It's especially useful for coaches to be able to listen in this way during coaching sessions. Or use it anytime you want to give someone a really good listening to!

Why would I do this? ➡ As your listening to other people improves, you will benefit from:
- A clearer understanding of other people, their situations, thoughts and issues.
- An ability to develop better rapport or relationship with others.
- A more relaxed style of conversation with others.

How long will it take? ➡ Approximately 45–60 minutes, depending on what the person you are working with wants to discuss.

Set-up

Ask your partner to think of three situations they'd like to create change around. These might be problems, minor frustrations, or goals and objectives they already have. If they can only think of a couple, that's OK – a third often pops up during the conversation. You are going to ask your partner to talk about each of the three situations or issues, one after another. Your role is that of listener, and your partner is the speaker.

The conversation – step by step

1 The speaker talks about their three things (problems or situations they want to change) with the listener. This should take about 30-40 minutes. During this time the listener may ask questions, acknowledge points raised, clarify information, etc.

2   The listener then takes about ten minutes to summarize back to the speaker:

➡ What the three issues or situations are.

➡ How the listener feels about them.

➡ What else seemed unspoken, yet present or relevant to the conversation.

3   Then the speaker gives the listener feedback, specifically:

➡ How 'listened to' did they feel, e.g. how well did they feel the listener gave them their full attention as they were speaking, and how well did they think the listener understood them?

➡ What effect did the listener's 'listening' have upon the speaker, e.g., 'It made me talk more, made me feel like this . . . etc'

➡ How did the exercise affect how the speaker now feels about the three things?

During feedback, the speaker should give both their experience, e.g. what they felt, and what caused that experience. For example, the speaker might say, 'I felt listened to because you asked me questions to help you understand what I was saying.'

It is important to observe specific behaviours that created a particular result or feeling, so that the person listening can begin to appreciate how other people experience their behaviours.

The role of the listener

The primary aim of the listener is to understand what the speaker is saying. By a process of listening, questioning or clarifying, you should aim to:

➡ Understand what the situations or problems really are, e.g. if they are not happy with their job, identify some of the causes of that. If they want a closer relationship with their step-children, find out the driving factors behind that, what is currently in the way, etc.

➡ Understand how they feel about the situations, and be able to tell them afterwards, e.g. 'I think this situation is frustrating you, and also perhaps upsetting you a little.'

➡ Be able to fill in gaps in the conversation, i.e. what wasn't said. For example, 'I think maybe you're wondering how your step-children's mother might react.'

Ground rules for the listener

During the conversation, however, **do not**:

➡ Attempt to give the speaker ideas, solutions or suggestions relating to the situations they are discussing.

➡ Refer to or discuss any of your own similar circumstances, experiences or feelings.

➡ Attempt to control the direction or content of the conversation.

➡ Seek to look good or impress the other person in any way, e.g. by asking 'clever' questions, by recalling tremendous amounts of information, etc.

Exercise Summary **Developing deep listening**

This exercise causes us to become aware of how much we are programmed to want to put 'something of ourselves' into a conversation with another person. We might do this by solving their problems for them, showing them how much we know about what they're talking about, or even taking over the conversation completely.

The exercise is great for developing a different listening perspective. The listener's only motive is to really understand and relate to the other person, nothing else.

Once this way of listening has been experienced, the listener can then practise this again and again, whenever they like. The other person doesn't have to know what they're doing, unless the listener wants feedback. At some point during their practices, the listener is likely to experience a greater sense of who the speaker is, how they feel, including those thoughts or feelings that aren't actually spoken. That's deep listening!

Skill three – using intuition

Building rapport
or relationship

Giving supportive
feedback

Coaching
skills

Different
levels of listening

Asking questions

Using intuition

Intuition – within coaching

Study any great coach and you will notice that they often seem to know in what direction to take a conversation, in order to gain information or insight that proves extremely relevant. The area they explore might appear unrelated and initially seem an odd thing to discuss. Subsequent conversation creates a real breakthrough in understanding or solutions for the coachee. This is one of the great distinguishing characteristics of a coach, and one that makes the coaching role so valuable.

Intuition is actually an ability we all have, and one we can develop into a skill.

Sometimes they may spot what's missing from the conversation, and become curious about something that's simply not being said. They may choose to ask a question, or make an observation that completely changes what's happening. From one simple remark or phrase, they may unlock an issue for someone or cast a whole new light on a situation. The way we explain this kind of behaviour is to call it intuition.

Intuition is actually an ability we all have, and one we can develop into a skill. For a coach, it becomes something they rely upon, to help shape and guide a coaching conversation.

The following dialogue illustrates such intuition:

COACH: 'So what is it about interviews that you don't like?'

COACHEE: 'Well, everything, I mean, the whole situation doesn't suit me. I get in there and everything seems to start going wrong.'

COACH: 'Perhaps say a little more about that . . .'

COACHEE: 'Well it's probably the questions, I know what I want to say it's just that my answers don't seem to flow in the right direction. I end up talking too much, about stuff that's irrelevant, sounding stupid. When I get out of there I realize I could have done so much better.'

COACH: 'You know, I keep wondering – who might you be proving right here?'

COACHEE: 'I don't understand what you mean.'

COACH: 'Well, who might expect you to behave like this at interviews?'

COACHEE: 'Aaah, that's easy, my dad I guess. He'd say I just couldn't cut it under pressure. My brother was always so much better at this sort of thing, I guess I kind of live in his shadow a little.'

You will see from the dialogue that there are several different ways the coach could have approached the situation, many of which would seem more logical. What happened is that during the conversation, the coach began to have thoughts and/or feelings that there was someone else involved in this issue. As well as someone else being involved, there was some sense of burden or resignation from the coachee. 'Who are you proving right here?' is not a stock question for a coach. The question simply came to the coach as a thought and they went with that thought and asked the question.

Intuition – wisdom in action

Intuition is simply an access to our brain's potential to provide guidance and information free from the confines of our limited conscious mind. Through intuition, we are able to access vast stores of experience, knowledge and wisdom in a way that sometimes defies logic. Intuition is a way our brain has of communicating with our conscious mind, and uses subtle means such as thoughts, feelings, sensations, imagery, sounds – or various combinations of those.

Intuition seems to be a function of both our brain and our body – think of how we talk about 'gut feelings', or 'having a feeling about something'. Intuition seems to potentially involve any part of our body, as it attempts to guide and direct our thoughts.

In the earlier example, the options for the next question were far too many for the coach to consider, assess and decide upon. Rational, practical thought would probably have explored techniques of great interview skills, preparing and rehearsing answers, investigating the interviewers beforehand, etc.

Even if the coach decided to analyze how the individual might be 'stopping' themselves from doing well during interviews, it would have taken a lot longer to logically arrive at the insight about the coachee's father. Instead the coach trusted a sense that someone was 'being proved right'. During coaching, this sometimes causes a coach to risk asking a dumb question, or receiving an uncomfortable response, e.g. 'I don't understand what you mean'. If the coach stays with his intuition, he'll continue until his curiosity is satisfied.

Communicating non-verbally

Intuition incorporates the brain's ability to understand communication from situations or people by going beyond the signals we normally respond to. Logically, we can respond to sight, sound, conversation, events, etc. I would also suggest that there are some forms of communication that happen where our conscious minds don't register them. It's a bit like dog whistles – we're simply not tuned into them. Our subconscious mind is able to gather, assess and interpret different kinds of information from people and situations.

I believe that we can communicate quite well without language – after all, animals are able to do so. For example, after walking into a room where two people have obviously been arguing, we say things like 'You could cut the air with a knife' – but what do we mean by that? We probably mean that we have picked up enough signals or communication from within the room to 'guess' that an argument has just taken place. If we were to try and explain exactly what signals we got that caused us to decide this, we can't always give a detailed answer. Maybe the two people were sitting quietly, maybe they weren't actually looking at each other – does that explain the atmosphere in the room?

The human brain is known to be an underestimated resource. Research suggests that we currently use less than 10 per cent of our brain's true potential. In other words, our brain is a lot smarter than we are. Whilst we struggle to compare more than three thoughts at a time, our brain's background processing is far superior.

I hear stories of doctors or emergency workers who need to – and can – assess a situation much more quickly and accurately than the conscious mind can. They often can't say exactly what led them to an almost instant certainty of what the person's problem was and what to do about it. Clearly, the brain is operating in a way in which we aren't aware of, in order to gain access to and compare information.

A practical tool

For me, there's nothing 'mystical' or 'spooky' about intuition; it's something that we all use, regularly and practically. Whether that's to choose the perfect present for someone, avoid scheduling something in our diaries because we have a feeling something else might crop up, or know someone's not telling us the truth. Intuition simply builds on what you already know – knowledge you already have that is communicated to you via thoughts, feelings, images or sounds.

How do we develop intuition?

Improving how we use our intuition takes practice. It may help you to begin by acknowledging how you already use it. How many decisions or choices do you currently make with minimal rational thought? What happens with you before you do? Call it instinct, call it a gut feeling – you already have it. How do you know when you've left the house and forgotten something? How do you know when someone's telling the truth or not?

Because intuition speaks to us using fairly subtle signals (imagery, feelings, sensations, thoughts, sounds, etc.), we have to learn to become more receptive to this form of communication.

Once you have an awareness of the forms of 'language' your subconscious is using, practise tuning in. In order to tune in, you need to work at creating a state of mind, body, breathing etc. that enables you to hear, feel, or imagine the messages coming from your subconscious. However, if you are feeling nervous, angry, excited, or your mind is simply full of other thoughts, you are unlikely to be able to open this channel for communication. Your strongest signals from intuition will come when you're feeling calm or relaxed.

An exercise **Using your own intuition**

Choose your next meal according to what your intuition is telling you. If you're in a restaurant, read down the list of options and ask yourself 'what's the best choice I could make here?' Settle into the question peacefully, and make sure you're relaxed in order to hear, feel or see the response. If you're relaxed, your breathing will be slightly slower, comfortable, and often you'll find yourself breathing from your stomach or mid-section.

This way of choosing food can actually be a good strategy for anyone wanting to eat more healthily or lose weight. Maintaining a relaxed state will give you access to your own wisdom. When your choice is based on this wisdom, you'll often find yourself choosing something that is a good choice for you and your body. Be warned you may end up eating something unusual!

The subtle nature of intuition

Intuition is not infallible; it is simply another source of thought and ideas. Because it is a subtle channel of information, it is easily interrupted, or drowned out, by the thoughts already going on in our conscious minds. It's a little like tuning in a radio to a particular station. If you get two at the same time, the louder one is the one we tend to focus on.

Ask yourself what you want to eat tonight and your conscious mind might shout 'choco-late!' or 'pizza!' loudly and repeatedly, every time you repeat the question. When your mind becomes peaceful and quiet, however, you may get the sense of a certain type of food or combination of foods, maybe with a higher water or protein content – chicken salad!

The pitfall of intuition

In my experience, intuition also gets things wrong, or at least seems to. For example, I don't seem to be able to pick winning horses at a racecourse using intuition. Now I don't know if that's because my intuition is failing me, or I'm simply not accessing it properly, or maybe my attachment to winning money distorts my ability in that setting. What I do know is a trip to the races usually costs me money! I would balance that by saying that I don't have any obvious knowledge or skill for picking horses. In other words, my sub-conscious mind has little information or experience with which to work.

What I am confident of is of my own ability to use intuition within a coaching environ-ment, because I do have both experience and developed skills in this area. I would suggest that the same is true for many individuals specializing within a particular field. For example, I bet a plumber can find a random fault in a heating system using his intu-ition faster than most of us. Based on years of experience and technical skill, what looks like magic is simply wisdom in action.

An implied need to develop our own learning

So if our intuition draws upon our latent wisdom and knowledge, then of course we benefit from increasing that knowledge. Continual learning and self-development will help a coach stay both effective and fresh. So whether you learn by reading, attending courses or seminars, debating with others, seeking feedback, listening to tapes, keeping a diary, studying others, or a combination of all those – I encourage you to remain both focused and committed to increasing your own knowledge and skill.

Skill four – asking questions

If the coach and the coachee are travelling companions, then the coach's questions and listening are the quality of light by which they travel.

Their answer is in your question

If the coach and the coachee are travelling companions, then the coach's questions and listening are the quality of light by which they travel.

The ability to ask fabulous questions consistently is uncommon enough to seem like a rare talent. It's actually a skill that can be developed, with concentration and practice. Within coaching, a beautifully timed, perfectly worded question can remove barriers, unlock hidden information and surface potentially life-changing insights. In other words, to be a great coach you need to be able to ask great questions.

What does a great question look like or sound like? Well, it will have the following characteristics:

⟹ it's simple;

⟹ it has a purpose;

⟹ it is influencing without being controlling.

Keeping things simple

Simple questions often have the greatest impact, because they allow the coachee to use energy forming their response, rather than trying to understand or follow the wording of the question. In addition, they often get 'to the heart of the matter' more easily, simply because of their direct nature. We obviously need to balance 'direct' with a need to maintain rapport, and that is still possible. When asking questions, being clever just isn't clever.

Complex questions confuse people

Unfortunately, for a coach, asking simple, straightforward questions isn't always automatic. Perhaps a coach hears their coachee say, 'Well, I need to earn more money you see – that's important'. The coach might decide that they want to understand the motivation behind that and so responds with the following complex question:

Too complex a question: 'When you consider your motivations, and what causes you to want to earn more money, what does this lead you to realize?'

This is not a great question. It's fairly long, and too complicated. The listener is asked to compare, analyze and then 'realize' something. There's also an implied pressure to come up with a particular 'realization', as though the coach knows the answer, and the coachee needs to come up with it. As a result of the coachee getting the answer 'wrong' or worse, not being able to produce an answer, the conversation may easily become uncomfortable or laboured.

Alternatively, the coach's next question might be:

Too casual a question: 'So what's all this earning more money about then?'

Again, not a great question. Although it's brief, it's also too casual and lacks focus. The response to this question may be equally flippant, e.g. 'Dunno – that's just me I guess.' Additionally, there's a subtle tone that suggests the individual is 'wrong' to want to earn more money. The phrasing is similar to that used by parents discussing a problem with their children: 'So what's all this noise/crying/fuss about then?' Again, when we make a person 'wrong' in the conversation, we begin to lose rapport.

Another 'simple' option might be:

Questioning 'why': 'Why do you want to earn more money?'

Easy to understand, fairly easy to respond to, but it contains the word 'why', which has risks associated with it. When we ask someone 'why' it can easily be interpreted as a request for them to justify themselves. When a person feels that pressure, they can easily become defensive and begin to form a 'logical' case for their own actions, e.g. 'Well, I just do, why should I put up with the lousy wages this place is paying me?'

Questions can be like keys that open doors

The best question is one that the coachee is willing to answer because it's both simple to understand and inoffensive in its tone. In addition, if the question is right, it will surface the information you both need to increase progress within the conversation. Suitable questions might include:

Simple questions with influence: 'Can you perhaps say a little more about how that's important.' This is a gentle, respectful question.

'What is it about earning more money that's important to you?' This is more direct, and relies on you having good rapport, and a fairly gentle tone of voice.

'So money's important – can you tell me a bit more about that?' A little more casual, a little less direct and still might easily hit the mark. If it doesn't, you can be sure it's going to get you closer.

In coaching, simply worded questions encourage the smooth flow of a conversation, as the coachee is able to concentrate on their thoughts, and respond naturally.

Questions with purpose

When we ask a question of someone, or even of ourselves, the question normally has purpose. For example, some questions gather information; some questions influence a person's thinking. Within coaching, the questions that a coach uses often do both.

Table 5.1 illustrates examples of good coaching questions, along with their purpose.

Table 5.1 Good coaching questions

Purpose	Coaching examples
Gather general information.	'Can you tell me more about what happened with her?' 'Could you say more about that?' 'What else is there to say about that?'
Gather specific information.	'Specifically, what was it about her that you didn't like?' 'Can you tell me what she actually said?' 'What words did she use that upset you?'
Help someone remember something more clearly.	'What can you remember about what happened?' 'What do you remember seeing/feeling/hearing?'
Shift someone's attention to the present moment, e.g. if they're becoming angry about something and you want them to relax a little.	'Okay, what else do you want to say about that to me right now?' 'So, what seems important about that right now?' 'Can you think of any other information that would be relevant about that for us here, now?'
Understand someone's values.	'What was it about her words that upset you?' 'What is important to you about that?' 'What would you have wanted her to say?' 'What do you value in a relationship?'

Purpose	Coaching examples
Help someone appreciate another person's values.	'What was important to her in this situation?' 'What might be her reasons for acting like that?'
Get someone to link two thoughts, or situations, together.	'How does the location you described relate to what happened?' 'How does this situation affect how you are at work now?'
Help someone appreciate something from someone else's perspective.	'What do you think her experience was?' 'What might she be feeling at that point?' 'What might her intention have been?'
Help someone come to a conclusion.	'What are your thoughts about that now?' 'What is the conclusion you are drawing about that now?'
Influence someone to action.	'What could you do about that right now?'
Prepare someone to overcome barriers to taking action.	'What might stop you from doing that?' (follow-up) 'So how will you overcome that?'
Influence someone to think about a situation positively.	'How have you benefited from this?' 'What will you get by sorting this whole matter out now?' 'What's the positive/up side of this?'

Purpose	Coaching examples
Influence someone to think about the effects of an action.	'What are the risks associated with your action?' 'How will this affect your other colleagues?' 'Who else is affected by this?'
Help someone gain learning from an event or circumstance.	'How has talking this through affected your views of this?' 'What learning have you taken from this?' 'How would you react if that kind of situation happened again?'

There are obviously lots of reasons to ask a question – too many to detail here. For a coach, it's important to decide in what direction to take a conversation, and then construct the appropriate question that fulfils that intent.

Occasionally, a coach will ask a question without really knowing why they've asked it. Where the question is based on instinct and experience, this is entirely appropriate. I would suggest, however, that this is the exception rather than the rule. To frequently ask random questions with no idea of their purpose would create a very strange conversation indeed!

Maintaining integrity of purpose

Questions may do many positive things in a conversation, such as create clarity, explore different perspectives, etc. Unfortunately they may also narrow options, imply judgement and leave the coachee feeling pressured or defensive.

It is important to make sure the purpose of a question is not corrupted by strong personal opinion. For example, a coach may hear a coachee describing his desire for a new job that involves more money and much more travel. The coach also knows that the coachee has recently said that his wife is expecting their first baby. Logically, it seems reasonable to look at the effect such a move may have on the person's family. The following questions may appear to do just that:

'Isn't that a bit unfair on your wife right now?'

'Won't that be difficult if your wife has just had a baby?'

Both questions, however, have an implied outcome and sense of judgement. The coach is expressing their own opinion by using words like 'difficult' and 'unfair'. The potential of exploring the effects of the job move is almost lost as the coachee is pressed to justify his statement.

With less of a sense of judgement, the following questions work better:

'How will a lot of travel affect things at home?'

'Who else will be affected by you changing jobs?'

By keeping the questions open and neutral the coachee can explore their own thoughts and awareness of the situation. This is an example of the non-directional approach outlined in Chapter 1, where the coach seeks to draw insights and learning from the coachee.

Influence 'vs' control – leading the witness

Asking someone a question automatically influences the direction of their thoughts. E.g. 'What was the best holiday you ever had?' causes you to think about holidays in the past.

Within coaching, a collaborative coach tries to maintain the balance between influence and control.

Although it subtly implies that you have had a great holiday at some point in your life, the question is fairly neutral, in that it doesn't tell you what you should think.

Within coaching, a collaborative (less directive) coach tries to maintain the balance between influence and control. Controlling questions can narrow down options, imply judgement, or create pressure on someone else to come up with the 'right' response. Perhaps when there's a time limit on a coach to reach a conclusion, these kinds of questions might be appropriate. Mostly, though, I'd discourage coaches from using them. Because they control thought and self-expression, the coach risks missing information, losing rapport, or both.

Table 5.2 illustrates controlling questions further.

Table 5.2 Controlling questions

Controlling question	Problem/Issue
'And what did you feel about that – frustrated?'	Narrows down options of what the person may have felt, plus subtly assumes what they 'should' have felt, i.e. frustrated.
'What caused you to act in such a hostile manner towards her?'	Implies both criticism and a requirement for the other person to justify their actions.
'How is that going to put things right if Kathy's still so upset?'	Again, implies disagreement and requests justification.
'What could you do to completely resolve the situation?'	Places pressure on the individual to get the question 'right' whilst implying subtle blame.
'What is it about Kathy that you aren't able to deal with?'	Assumes that the other person isn't able to deal with Kathy, and that's a bad thing.

Making someone wrong

One other thing common to most of the above questions is that they make the other person wrong in some way for their actions. By making someone 'wrong' for something, we create difference or distance between us, e.g. 'Don't you think that was a little silly?'

When a coach frequently makes a coachee wrong, they risk damaging rapport and the ongoing relationship.

Table 5.3 gives more neutral alternatives.

Table 5.3 Neutral questions

Coaching question	Benefit
'How did you feel about that?'	Open question, enables the coachee to decide how they felt.
'What caused you to do that?' 'What was behind the way you acted towards her?'	Helps the coachee disassociate in order to identify reasons for their behaviour.
'What effect will doing that have upon Kathy do you think?'	Helps the coachee see the implications of their actions for others.
'What might you do to help the situation?'	Allows the coachee to consider various ways of helping, plus imagining themselves doing them.
'What is it about Kathy's behaviour that's important to you?'	Distinguishes Kathy's behaviour from Kathy the person. Also, uses the word 'important' in a way that implies no judgement.

The importance of voice

Any question is given further meaning by the quality of your voice when you ask it. Questions may be made clearer, colder, more supportive or more aggressive simply by the tone, warmth and speed of your voice.

An exercise **Use your voice**

Using the question 'So what was important about that?' repeat it three different times, changing the quality of your voice each time, using the following characteristics:

➡ With a cruel sneer.

➡ With sarcasm (and end with a sigh!).

➡ With genuine curiosity, as though the answer is important to you.

You will notice that a great question can be completely wrecked by the wrong tonality.

Also, use great tonality with a potentially risky or abrupt question, and you're more likely to get a good response.

An appreciation of closed and open questions

Part of the flexibility a coach needs to develop can be found in the effective use of both closed and open questions. Closed questions can be answered with a 'yes' or 'no', and open questions can't:

➡ Closed questions (Y/N):
  – Did you enjoy that?
  – Would you like this?
  – Can you do that?
  – Will that be here by Friday?
  – Is that everything?

➡ Open questions:
  – What did you enjoy about that?
  – Who would like this?
  – How can we get this done?
  – When will it be delivered?
  – What else is there?

Open questions encourage more information than closed. They also encourage participation and involvement in the conversation, and allow us to explore someone else's thoughts and ideas. For this reason, a good coach will tend to use many more open questions than closed. During a typical coaching session I would expect the coachee to be doing at least 70 per cent of the talking. Using open questions is one way a coach can achieve this.

Nevertheless, closed questions may still be used to great effect, especially where we don't want a detailed response, e.g:

Confirming information	'Have I got that right?'
Moving the conversation along	'Can we continue?'
Closing a conversation down	'Have we finished?'

The exception is when people don't respond to closed questions with a yes or no – this is especially common with politicians!

Coach's corner

Q What if I can't think of my next question?

Sometimes a coach will go blank, get stuck, and not know what to say next! This is normal, human and happens to all coaches that I know of. Causes and potential options include:

The coach has lost concentration and has lost the thread of the conversation

Be honest, declare what's happened, and move on, e.g. 'I'm really sorry, I need you to repeat what you just said, I lost concentration just then.' Then make sure you refocus on the conversation and what the coachee is saying, in order to regain your involvement.

The coach is genuinely distracted by another thought, idea or insight

Be honest, declare what's happening, e.g. 'I'm sorry, but I keep thinking about what you said earlier about not liking things too easy, can we go back to that a little?' It might be that your intuition has made a connection that's worth exploring.

The conversation seems to be leading nowhere or seems 'stuck', e.g. maybe the energy has gone out of the conversation, or the conversation feels pointless

Be honest (again!). Say what you're feeling or thinking – after all, they might be thinking it too. For example, 'OK, I'm kind of stuck now because I don't know where our conversation is heading – is this still a useful discussion?' They might say 'Yes I'm actually getting a lot from this,' So if they think it's still useful, find out how, e.g. 'Help me understand a little more about that.' You'll then have a new focus for the conversation.

Alternatively, if they say 'I know what you mean, I'm stuck with it as well', you can then decide how it's best to continue, e.g. 'OK – do we leave that or do we want to know why we've got stuck with it?' or 'OK, what could we be talking about?'

The coach's mind has simply gone blank because they are nervous or new to coaching

This one is helped by a little advance preparation. Learn to relax yourself and refocus. Perhaps use your body to help you regain your sense of inner calm and confidence. Maybe sit back a little, pull your shoulders back, and move your breathing down into your stomach (so that your tummy goes in and out as you breathe). Use a 'holding' phrase to enable you to refocus your thoughts, e.g. 'I'm pausing a little here, I just want to think about what you've just said' (then focus onto what they've just said). Remember that pauses are often useful for the coachee as well as the coach – silences can be powerful! Alternatively, do a brief recap, using your notes if you have them, e.g. 'Let's just recap a little, we've begun by saying that we wanted to. . .' Usually this is enough to re-orientate you to the conversation, helping you decide what you want to explore or discuss.

Powerful questions

Powerful questions have many potential benefits, for example:

➡ They refocus thought, e.g. from problem to solution.

➡ They can help someone feel more powerful and constructive about a situation.

➡ They tap into creativity and create options.

➡ They can make a problem feel more like a challenge or an opportunity.

➡ They create forward movement, i.e. out of the problem state and into solution or action.

Powerful questions are phrased in such a way to encompass the problem and provoke an answer. The answer that they produce addresses the deeper problem, not just the surface issue. Table 5.4 demonstrates the journey between describing a situation as a problem and describing the same situation with a powerful question. The particular situation here is that the person is overworked and wants more support from their boss. They feel that their boss doesn't know much about their day-to-day situation and doesn't value the workload they are carrying.

Table 5.4 Using powerful questions

Statement/Question	Comment
'I'm really struggling with this job, and my boss doesn't support me – he doesn't even know what I do!'	This is a statement of complaint or problem; it focuses on what's wrong. It's not a question, and it produces no creative thoughts or ideas.
'Why can't my boss help me?'	This is a question, but it's not a powerful question. It's actually still a complaint. Also, if this question were answered, we'd get responses like 'because he's not interested/too busy, etc.' Such responses are not going to progress this issue.
'How can I get my boss to know more about what I'm doing?'	This question covers only the superficial aspect of the problem and so evokes only a partial answer. Remember that the person also wants their boss to support them, not just be aware of what they do. Responses to this question might include 'Spend some time with him so that he understands what you do.' A powerful question will produce answers to the deeper problem.
'How can I make sure my boss understands more about what I'm doing, and encourage him to give me more support?'	This is a good, powerful question. The question digs below the surface, in order to bring up a complete solution. The likely response would create ideas that address all parts of the problem, i.e. make the boss aware, and get him to support more.

As soon as we present a really powerful question around a situation, you can almost hear minds crunch into gear. It's as if the human brain can't resist the challenge of a really juicy question. For example, imagine you've been complaining relentlessly about needing a holiday but also needing the money to fix your car. You hate the car, you'd prefer something smaller, but it seems too much hassle to change it. Then someone asks you:

'How can you have *both* the car you want and the holiday you need?'

Hmm – gets you thinking, doesn't it?

Powerful questions are an invaluable tool within coaching.

Powerful questions are an invaluable tool within coaching, and good coaches will ask them in a variety of situations. Perhaps the coachee is complaining repeatedly and not progressing towards a solution. Or maybe the coachee is blaming their situation on other people or things. Powerful questions often shift people's attention to a more powerful, responsible perspective. In addition, they introduce the possibility of a solution in the mind of a coachee where previously none existed.

Table 5.5 shows some more examples of powerful questions.

Table 5.5 More powerful questions

Coachee's statement	Powerful question
'I've moved jobs, I've moved home and now I've got no friends and no social life – it makes the whole thing seem pointless somehow.'	'What could you be doing to feel more settled and meet some new friends?'
'I'm always worried about money, I'm worried about it regardless of how much I have. It's just always in my thoughts.'	'What's it going to take for you to feel relaxed about money?'
'I want to go to night school but there's no one reliable to look after the kids, the situation's just impossible.'	'How can you get someone reliable to look after the kids while you go to night school?'

Often, people get bogged down by their complaints about how bad things are, or about how difficult their problems are, and never progress to sorting things out. In coaching, powerful questions can be a really effective way of moving someone forward from a problem, to a solution and action. This is a natural part of the coaching role, and can be of great value to the person being coached.

An exercise | **Powerful questions**

The following will help you to experience powerful questions:

Step one – identify three problem statements

Write down three problems that you think you have. Choose things that are moderately important but not earth-shattering, e.g. 'I don't have enough time to exercise.' Leave enough space under each statement to write a few more sentences.

Step two – change problem statements into powerful questions

Under each problem, write down questions that provoke solutions to the issue, e.g. 'How can I create more time to exercise?' Remember, for a question to be powerful it must have the following attributes:

➡ The question assumes that there is an answer to the problem.

➡ The question provokes thought to begin to create answers or solutions.

➡ The question digs below the surface, and thereby invites a more encompassing solution.

For further support, look back at the previous examples.

Step three – answer your own questions!

On a clean piece of paper, write your powerful questions down one side. Then, focusing on each question, produce ideas or solutions, e.g. 'Get up an hour earlier', 'Ask Jon to pick the kids up from school sometimes', 'Prepare more food for the freezer on weekends.'

Once you have some really great solutions, simply decide which you're going to commit to!

What if your question doesn't create progress?

Sometimes, no matter how many great questions a coach might ask a coachee, the coachee is simply stuck and can't progress in the conversation. For example, a coach asks 'What else could you have done in that situation?' and the coachee simply can't think of an answer. The coach has asked the question because they want the coachee to understand their options, or perhaps produce some learning from a situation. The coach would prefer that the learning came from the coachee if possible. However, the coachee appears not to be able to think of anything as a response. In this instance, a coach has the following options:

➡ Does the coachee need more time or silence in order to respond?

➡ Is there another, similar question that might help them, e.g. 'What options did you have?' or 'What would Zorro do?' (OK maybe not Zorro, but someone else, then.)

➡ Is there something else bothering them that needs to be addressed before they can continue, e.g. 'Are you comfortable discussing this right now?'

Give an observation before an answer

If the above options still fail to create progress, the coach may be tempted to just give the coachee an answer, e.g. 'Well, you could have spoken to your manager about your plans first.' For reasons discussed previously, this may not be the best way to promote learning for the coachee, plus the coach might get the answer wrong. There is, however, a useful step towards giving an answer.

The coach has the option of first making an observation, as a way of encouraging the coachee's thinking process. Using the earlier example, the following observations may all be relevant:

➡ 'What you did was to prepare the report by yourself then introduce it at the meeting.'

➡ 'The report came as quite a surprise to everyone didn't it?'

➡ 'Well, you said that the report didn't get the response you wanted, and I was wondering what else you might have done to make sure that it was well received.'

That last seems to work particularly well, as it combines an observation with a nice, gentle question.

So it's important to remember that just because a coachee can't answer a question quickly and easily, the coach still has options. A period of silence, asking another question or making an observation can all encourage further thoughts and ideas.

> **Exercise summary** **Asking questions**
>
> The ability to ask great questions is one of the most important skills a coach develops. Great questions are simple to answer, give direction to the conversation and gently influence someone else's thinking. A simply worded question, delivered at the appropriate moment, can shift or shape someone's thinking dramatically.

Skill five – giving supportive feedback

Feedback as a way of learning

One of the great things about a coaching relationship is that it helps the coachee to experience a different view of themselves and their situations. One obvious way that they experience this view is through the eyes of the coach. The coach is able to give their own views of the coachee and so contribute to the coachee's picture of themselves and their experience. This might range from simple encouraging observations, to more challenging views of the coachee's attitudes or behaviours.

The ability of a coach to give their own views of a coachee constructively is important to the coaching experience.

The ability of a coach to give their own views of a coachee constructively is important to the coaching experience. Effective feedback can accelerate a coachee's learning, inspire and motivate them, help them feel valued and literally catapult them into action! So it's important that a coach learns to deliver feedback that is:

➡ Given with a positive intention.

➡ Based on fact or behaviour.

➡ Constructive and beneficial.

(We will examine these characteristics of feedback in more detail later in the chapter.)

What do we mean by feedback?

The term feedback means literally to feed information back to someone. This information relates to the person receiving the feedback and provides data from which they can assess their performance or experiences. It can range from a general comment such as 'That was great/lousy' to more specific assessments of performance such as 'You had your hand an inch too high.'

Many of us are familiar with the term feedback, maybe from situations at work, or learning situations, e.g. school or college. In recent years, the term has unfortunately become associated with criticism, due to how and when people choose to use it. The expression 'I'd like to give you some feedback' is sometimes used as an introduction to a fairly negative conversation. This is especially common in business, where praise and encouragement are rare, and frustrations or disputes must be handled 'professionally'. By using the word 'feedback', individuals are able to give the illusion of professionalism to critical remarks.

It's a shame, because whilst critical remarks do constitute feedback (they're information), often the same message could be delivered in a more supportive and probably effective manner. For example, the following statements all relate to the same situation:

'You keep upsetting people because you're so blunt with your remarks.'

'When you told Mark he'd no chance of getting the job, I thought he appeared upset.'

'When you told Mark he'd no chance of getting the job, how do you think he felt?'

All three comments have the same intention, i.e. to change the way in which the person speaks to others.

The first remark sounds like generalized, subjective criticism, and may easily upset the person hearing it. This remark is not a supportive way of giving someone feedback.

The second remark comments on specific behaviour in a more objective way, and is less likely to offend the individual. The remark is fairly direct, although within a healthy coaching relationship this level of openness should be OK.

The third option uses a question to explore the impact upon the person, Mark. This is a much less direct attempt to influence someone's behaviour. This is not feedback, although it is a valid option to meet the objective of influencing the coachee's future behaviour.

Knowing when to give feedback

Within coaching, there are no hard and fast rules as to when to give feedback but there are guidelines. An opportunity for feedback may be prompted either by the coach or the coachee. In either instance, the coach should offer feedback only in the genuine belief that it would benefit the coachee.

Potential benefits for the coachee when they receive feedback include:

➡ It has a positive impact on their learning.

➡ It offers useful information or perspectives.

➡ It encourages or motivates the coachee.

➡ It confirms or compares views and opinions.

➡ It prompts insights or ideas.

Sometimes, the coachee simply hasn't noticed something, is avoiding considering something or is simply stuck in their own thoughts. At these times, using feedback is often a good choice to make. By intervening with a piece of well-timed feedback, the coach can often clarify thoughts, offer alternative views and even unblock blockages.

Sometimes, coachees will look for reassurance and say things like 'I bet you think I'm mad, don't you?' or 'Do you think I'm being silly about this?' In this instance, the coachee is probably looking for some simple reassurance before continuing talking. In cases like this it's easier for the coach to make a quick comment like 'No, of course I don't. Carry on . . .'

If a coachee asks for feedback and a coach is not willing to give it the coachee can easily become uncomfortable. The situation might be more important, e.g. 'I just don't seem to be making progress with this, why do you think that is?' If the coach refuses to comment, the coachee may view this as a withdrawal of some kind. The coachee might even become slightly paranoid, as they begin to suspect the coach has formed negative thoughts or judgements about them.

As a balance, there are some occasions where it would not be relevant to give feedback. For instance:

➡ Where it seems to be an excuse for the coachee to avoid taking responsibility, e.g. 'What do **you** think about all this?'

➡ If, giving feedback, the coach interrupts the flow of a conversation or the thought processes of the coachee.

➡ If giving feedback may lead to an inappropriate level of control by the coach, e.g. 'Let me tell you what I think about your situation.'

➡ Where the coach does not have enough information to give feedback effectively, e.g. 'Well I could guess what might be happening is . . .'

Imagine you are coaching someone who appears overly concerned with what other people think, and it affects their ability to make decisions. Their first thought is to check what other people might say or feel about what they do before fully exploring what they themselves want. In the past, this has led to them missing out on opportunities, or suffering in silence instead of expressing their views and needs. A coaching dialogue on this might sound as follows:

COACH: 'So what will you do about the job offer?'

COACHEE: 'Well, I'm not sure. I've been asking around, doing a bit of a survey. Trouble is, everyone seems to be saying different things. I mean, you know me, and what I'm good at – do you believe I'm capable of doing it?'

COACH: 'Well, I can easily add my view, but what I'm really interested in is what you believe.'

COACHEE: 'What I think? Well, I'm not sure I've thought about that!'

It is appropriate for the coach to challenge the coachee's tendency to place too much importance on what other people think. In this way, they encourage the coachee to use a different decision-making strategy that relies more on what they themselves think and feel.

The decision when or whether to give feedback should be based on a balance of the potential benefits and risks of doing so. Whilst the risks are rarely significant in isolated instances, over time continual feedback can result in the coach taking too much authority within the coaching relationship.

The coach simply needs to balance the pros and cons of giving feedback and to act accordingly.

How to give feedback

As we mentioned earlier, feedback should be:

➡ Given with a positive intention.

➡ Based on fact and behaviour.

➡ Constructive and beneficial.

The person hearing feedback that is clumsily worded and badly delivered can experience it as criticism, e.g. 'You're being arrogant about this'. This can usually be avoided by the person giving feedback taking care about what they say, and how they say it. Some people will be more receptive to hearing feedback than others, and a coach must develop the ability to deliver a potentially difficult message in such a way as to maintain the motivation of the coachee.

Some people will be more receptive to hearing feedback than others.

Of course, not all feedback is related to difficult messages. Praise and acknowledgement of good performance or progress is equally as important as observations of someone's need to adopt change, or develop different behaviours. Where messages are positive in nature, the previous principles of intention, based on behaviour, fact etc. still apply.

I would add that whilst the following guidelines apply within a coaching relationship, they also work for anyone giving feedback outside a coaching situation.

Feedback given with a positive intention

There are both positive and negative reasons to give someone feedback. For example:

➡ Positive reasons:
  - To help the individual learn something that they would benefit from learning.
  - To support the individual to reach their goal or objective.
  - To help the individual overcome a problem that's bothering them.
  - To acknowledge them; make them feel valued.

➡ Negative reasons:
  - To 'teach someone a lesson'.
  - To gain favour with someone else, i.e. not the individual.
  - To help someone else avoid giving feedback, i.e. doing it for them.
  - To control or dominate someone else, e.g. telling them what they should do.

Once our intention is clear and positive towards the individual, we are more likely to deliver a message that they experience as respectful and supportive. If it's a difficult message to deliver, sometimes by first speaking our intention we can help the individual to appreciate the potential benefit of listening to it. For example:

> COACH: 'I'd like to give you some feedback, as I know you've been experiencing some frustration with the lack of support you say you've gotten from your colleagues. I think I've noticed something that may help you gain a fresh perspective on that.'

The coach's intention is clearly positive towards the individual, and they are being very open about that. The coachee is likely to hear any information that follows with a degree of positive expectation.

A need for integrity

Personal judgements, frustrations, or a need to gain control of a situation may all corrupt a coach's ability to deliver really great feedback. For example, at the end of a very full day's coaching, the final session is running over time, and the coach is conscious that she's going to miss her train home. The coachee is slowly deliberating over a decision and there's silence in the room. The coach interrupts with:

> COACH: 'Can I give you some feedback?'
>
> COACHEE: 'Err – Okay . . .'
>
> COACH: 'You seem to be procrastinating. I think you simply need to take the decision now and then stick to it.'

If the coach were honest, she'd admit that her comment was borne out of frustration, and her intention was to control the conversation by bringing it to a close. This is not an intention that's going to benefit the effectiveness of the coaching, or the coaching relationship. The remark might upset both the coachee's feelings and their decision-making process.

Given the coach's frustration and her need to close the session, this was not the place to use the mechanism of feedback. An acknowledgement of the time, and a request to adjourn the conversation would probably have worked better.

Feedback based on fact and behaviour

Feedback is more likely to be effective if it is factual, and based on something the individual can do something about or change. Usually it's best to comment on behaviour, as a person can appreciate that they have choices about how they behave. Feedback that's non-specific or vague leaves them guessing, e.g. 'You're not doing that right, are you?', or 'You need to get better at that.'

Feedback that relates to who someone is, i.e. their identity, is also difficult. Whilst changing behaviour is fairly straightforward, changing who we are seems impossible. For example:

> 'Well, the presentation didn't go well, did it? That was because you're someone who tries too hard. That became obvious during the question and answer session.'

This remark is too general, too vague for the person hearing it to do much with. They are left with the option of being someone who 'doesn't try so hard' – which may not be something they can do anything about.

Within the same situation, the following feedback is more useable, and so likely to be more effective:

> 'I noticed that some of your answers to the questions were quite long and I suspect that caused some people to lose the sense of what you were saying.'

This is an observation of behaviour, plus a personal opinion of the effect of that behaviour. The person hearing it can disassociate from their behaviour enough to evaluate the situation more objectively. After all, most people know how to stop talking.

As a more positive example, if I notice that the coachee smiled a lot at the audience and that they responded by smiling back a lot, I can give the coachee that observation. In future, they can choose to repeat the behaviour, in the knowledge that it's likely to produce a good result.

The difference between objective and subjective feedback

Within coaching it's useful to understand the difference between a statement that is objective and one that is subjective. Objective statements are based solely on fact, e.g. something that actually happened. Subjective statements contain the views and opinions of an individual person. For example:

Example 1 Objective	[Coach]	'Before you said yes to that question, you paused and smiled.'
Example 2 Subjective	[Coach]	'Before you said yes to that question, you paused and smiled – for me, that's real progress.'

The first statement comments only on behaviour, making it more objective. The fact that the coach chose to observe the behaviour at all suggests they think it is significant, and that requires some judgement – but for the purposes of coaching, we'd still consider it an objective statement. The coach simply makes the observation to enable the coachee to respond with their own thoughts. The coachee is likely to comment on what caused them to pause and smile.

The second statement obviously adds the coach's opinion that progress is being made. The coach intends the statement to be supportive and encouraging and the coachee is more likely to respond to the encouragement, e.g. with 'Thanks' or 'Great'.

Whilst both statements are very similar in nature, notice that in their subtle difference they may create a very different result. However, I'd like to be really clear that neither form of feedback is right or wrong. What is important is that we appreciate the varying degrees to which we are being subjective or objective. The amount of fact and personal opinion within our statements affects the potential benefits, risks and results of feedback.

Subjective – the pros and cons

There are both benefits and risks attached to the coach giving subjective feedback.

Potential risks include being wrong and directing or controlling the coachee in an inappropriate manner. By using their own views and opinions, e.g. 'I think', the coach is introducing a form of guidance which might be directive.

This risk of over-influencing the coachee must be balanced with the potential benefits of providing support, acknowledgement and recognition. Once the coach has established both credibility and rapport with the coachee, their input is often welcome. Over a period of time, the coach gains valuable insight into the behaviours and tendencies of the coachee that might help them to progress towards their goals.

Again, it's a question of balance and a need to avoid extremes, i.e. too many personal views or no input at all. In practice, I tend to avoid giving personal views where possible as in general they get in the way of an individual's ability to find their own solutions.

Objective – the pros and cons

Objective statements reduce the coach's influence to a minimum, and allow the coachee to respond only to facts. Of course these 'facts' rely on the ability of the coach to observe behaviour correctly, or else the whole process is flawed.

Objective, factual statements are more likely to be accepted by the coachee as 'true' than are statements heavily laden with the coach's opinion. With the former, there's less non-factual information to debate. For example, if I say 'You raised your eyebrows when I said that' as opposed to 'You don't believe me, do you?' the first observation is more easily accepted than the other.

The potential down side of the coach making only objective, factual statements is that the coachee may actually need the coach's personal input to progress. Some behaviour might benefit from the coach interpreting it, e.g. 'I sense that you're avoiding discussing your current partner' might work better than 'You've talked a lot about your previous marriage.'

The next example illustrates the journey between objective and subjective feedback. The following coachee has a goal of being more influential in meetings.

Example 1   [Coach]   'You said that you take notes throughout the meetings.'

This is fairly objective, although obviously there is some judgement implied by the fact that the coach has chosen to focus on the behaviour at all.

Example 2   [Coach]   'You take notes a lot. That might be related.'

Still fairly objective and has a hint of the coach's views.

Example 3   [Coach]   'You take notes a lot. That's going to affect your influence.'

This is less objective, and contains more of the coach's views.

Example 4   [Coach]   'You take too many notes. It's got to be causing you to lack personal impact.'

A fairly hefty amount of personal opinion – subjective feedback – in this one.

Example 5   [Coach]   'Because you're taking notes all the time, it's causing you to lack presence. This is what's really affecting the situation.'

This is an extremely subjective statement that suggests strong opinion on the part of the coach. It's also very risky, as the coach is making a statement based on their understanding of the situation, which is limited to their knowledge. Also, by suggesting that taking notes is the most important factor, Example 5 controls the direction of the conversation too much.

Remember, collaborative coaching is a less directive, less controlling style of conversation. That way, we place primary responsibility for the conversation and the situation with the coachee.

The coach needs to decide whether to give a simple objective observation as feedback, or subjective feedback containing more of their own opinion. The following dialogue illustrates:

[Coachee] 'I don't know, maybe I'm worrying too much about the whole situation. What do you think about all this?'

Now at this point, the coach has options:

➡ Decline to give input and simply continue seeking to understand the situation, e.g. ' Well, what I'm really interested in is how you feel about it – what do you think?'

➡ Offer a simple objective feedback, e.g. ' Hmm, well, we have been discussing this for most of the session.'

➡ Offer subjective feedback, such as 'Well, the discussion does seem to be a little out of proportion to the problem. It sounds to me like you're worrying unnecessarily.'

Again, there are no right or wrong options – only outcomes. It is important that the coach appreciates they have a choice of response and they should choose according to their desired result.

An exercise | **Who's being objective?**

This exercise is a bit of fun with a twist. You'll need your favourite newspaper or magazine and a piece of paper and a pen. Choose a fairly brief article you're interested in reading. Read the article once, so that you understand what's in it. Now, divide your paper into two columns, one headed 'objective' and the other 'subjective'. Using the columns, separate the objective facts in the article from the subjective or opinion-based statements. When you've finished, notice what and how much is in each column.

Q What does that say about your preferred reading material?

Feedback that is constructive and beneficial

Within coaching, if a piece of feedback is effective, then it will benefit the coachee in some way. The feedback may create deeper understanding, build an idea, encourage productive action or simply increase someone's sense of well-being.

Being constructive also relates to how the coachee experiences the feedback. One of the signs of a good coach is their ability to make a potentially difficult or awkward message easier for the coachee to hear and experience. In order to make this happen, the coach must maintain the emotional state of the coachee throughout the feedback conversation. To do this, a good coach will often:

⇒ Balance difficult messages with positive statements.

⇒ Take personal responsibility for the views he/she is giving, e.g. 'I notice' or 'I think.'

⇒ Use open questions to encourage the coachee to shift perspectives or explore other avenues of thought.

⇒ Use neutral or diminished emphasis of words and phrases to describe difficult situations or emotions, e.g. some discomfort, slight resistance, etc.

⇒ Communicate supportively using non-verbal signals, e.g. posture, facial expressions, tonality, eye contact, etc.

⇒ Link observations to goals, e.g. 'This may help you to approach your time management a little differently.'

For the coachee to judge the feedback as constructive, the conversation must be, in balance, positive to them. They must feel that the coach has their success and well-being at heart, and that it was a worthwhile conversation to have in support of their ongoing development. For this reason, the coach must be able to deliver messages and observations in a way that the coachee accepts. By effectively combining the above principles of style and delivery, the coachee is more likely to welcome the feedback as constructive.

Balance difficult messages with positive statements.

Clearly, there must be some benefit to the feedback conversation for the coachee. Where feedback is directly related to the coachee's goals, this is fairly straightforward. Where the feedback does not obviously relate to the coachee's goals, the coach should establish a relevant benefit when considering their intent for giving feedback.

Coach's corner

Q What if my feedback gets a negative response?

Sometimes, we find our feedback isn't received in the way we wanted it to be. Maybe the coachee responds in a way we feel is negative. Responses we hadn't hoped for might include the coachee being upset, angry, unpleasantly surprised, or maybe they simply reject the feedback given completely. Causes of negative responses to feedback can vary, from an unsupportive statement clumsily delivered, to a simple misunderstanding of what's been said. Maybe as a coach we're not feeling great ourselves, maybe we're feeling pressured, stressed or just tired (these are not good times to give feedback by the way!). Or maybe we don't understand enough about the person or their situation to attempt offering feedback. There may be an external factor that affects their response. For example, we use a phrase or word that they are already very sensitive to like 'dominant' and this creates an overly defensive reaction. There are a number of principles that can support a coach if this should happen, namely:

Immediately after the coachee's response

Make sure that this is a genuinely negative response that you need to act upon:

For example, what you decide is a 'stony silence' might simply be the time the coachee needs to consider what they've just heard. Perhaps re-play in your mind what's just happened, and consider other possible causes of their response. Alternatively, if the coachee begins protesting, or becomes angry or upset, then listen to what they say before you decide what you need to do. If you know that your feedback has been clumsily delivered, then focus on making amends.

Take full responsibility for your unsupportive feedback

Acknowledge that your feedback hasn't worked out the way you intended. Apologize and accept that you have regret about causing their response, for example:

'I'm sorry, I've upset you and I didn't mean to.'

'I've upset you with what I've said, I'm sorry, that's my fault.'

'I'm now really regretting putting it like that, I'm sorry.'

If you're not sure what it was you said that caused the upset, then still acknowledge your responsibility, e.g. 'I think I've upset you with what I've just said – have I?'

If you find you're actually not responsible, then simply stay supportive of the coachee, e.g. by allowing them time to think, or listening to why they've reacted in the way they have.

Make amends, explain if possible/appropriate

Explain your intentions, but don't excuse yourself, stay responsible. For example: 'My intention was to be helpful but I haven't been have I?' or 'I wanted to give you another way of looking at the situation, I hoped that might give you another way forward.'

After the session

While maintaining responsibility for causing the response, seek to understand what it was you did that caused it and learn from the experience. Your options for learning include:

➡ When the coachee is in an appropriate state of mind, ask them to help you understand what you did that didn't work. Be careful to maintain a position of full responsibility, and ask them to help you learn. Be prepared to explain your intentions, but avoid justifying yourself or making excuses.

➡ Review the situation with someone you trust to help you learn from the situation, (whilst maintaining the confidentiality of the coachee).

➡ Read this chapter again, and consider what principles or methods might have enabled you to give the feedback in such a way as to create a better response.

Coach's corner

If we're going to learn to give feedback we're going to make mistakes. So it's important to know the principles of giving good feedback and focus on them. Where we give feedback that is unsupportive, then we need to acknowledge that and make amends if possible. Then we need to learn from the experience. And please don't let a bad experience of giving feedback stop you from ever giving any more – the world needs you to be great at giving fabulous feedback!

An example of constructive feedback

Obviously the non-verbal element of giving constructive feedback cannot be demonstrated here. The other principles are, however, illustrated in the following dialogue:

COACH: 'I wanted to discuss a little more your desire for less tension at home, which is proving a little more difficult now you've got your parents staying for a few months.'

COACHEE: 'A little difficult? – You can say that again!'

COACH: 'I've noticed that when you're speaking about your mother mostly it's a complaint, for example, "She's so moody" or "She just loves being difficult."'

COACHEE: 'Right – yes I suppose that's true.'

COACH: 'The other thing that seems to relate to this is the way you portray your father in the situation.'

COACHEE: 'How's that?'

COACH: 'Well, you sound like you care for your father a lot. When you discuss him in relation to your mother, you say things like "Poor guy, I don't know how he copes with her" and "She must make his life misery."'

COACHEE: 'Yeah, I guess I do feel pretty sorry for him.'

Notice how the coach is gradually constructing a picture of the situation that the coachee finds it easy to accept. Observations so far are mainly objective, i.e. facts about behaviour.

In addition, the coach is careful not to use emotive or potentially sensational words that might cause the coachee to be uncomfortable or defensive. For example, instead of saying something like 'You don't want going home to be such a nightmare', the coach chooses to say 'You want less tension at home.' It's a subtle distinction and an important trick to use sometimes.

The same dialogue continues:

COACH: 'You know, I'm wondering if how you discuss the situation is affecting how you're responding to it, and perhaps how you're feeling about it.'

COACHEE: 'Okay – go on.'

COACH: 'What effect could that be having on you do you think?'

COACHEE: 'Well I guess I'm thinking about it more, I certainly seem to be discussing it with anyone who will listen. I guess I'm making the whole thing worse.'

COACH: 'Okay, so I hear you complaining about your mother yet discussing your father as someone to feel sorry for or sympathize with. How does this actually affect your behaviour at home with them?'

COACHEE: 'Hmm, now I'm getting it. That's not a nice thought, actually. I'm seeing how I am around my parents at home and it does mirror what I say. I'm very different around my father than I am around my mother.'

COACH: 'How's that?'

COACHEE: 'Well, much more patient I guess.'

COACH: 'And is there an opportunity here?'

COACHEE: 'Yeah – I need to work out how I'm really featuring in all this – that's the opportunity to affect the whole thing, isn't it?'

Notice from the dialogue how the coach carefully constructs an increased awareness of the situation in collaboration with the coachee. Open questions are used to both involve and engage the coachee in the conversation. Gradually, the coachee builds a fresh perspective on the situation that enables them to create other options for a way forward.

Remember the importance of maintaining the coachee's emotional state. This includes not upsetting them unnecessarily or putting them on their guard. In general, an understatement is more likely to be accepted than an exaggeration. Within coaching I tend to use caution when describing situations. It's easier for a coachee to hear 'You have a situation that you want to change' than 'You've got a big problem here.'

An exercise Get some feedback

A great way to learn about giving feedback is for you to experience receiving some. That way you can learn about what works and what does not work, plus how it actually feels to be focused on in this way. To do the exercise, choose someone who knows you well (who you like and trust). As a word of caution, the intention of this this exercise is for you to experience feedback. There can be no guarantees that you'll like what you hear, or agree with what's said. Remember, to give supportive feedback yourself, you need to know what works and what doesn't.

Part one – set-up

You're going to ask this person for some feedback on a particular topic that you feel comfortable discussing, for example:

➡ What kind of manager am I?

➡ What kind of parent am I?

➡ How am I at giving presentations/running meetings, etc.?

Or any other area that you're interested in getting better at. If you're interested in a stretch, ask them to think about how they experience you generally, as a person.

Part two –the questions

Ask them to consider the following three questions, with regard to the topic or area you've requested feedback on:

Q What am I good at?/What do I do well?/What are my strengths, etc.?

Q What am I not so good at?

Q What could I do differently to improve?

When your partner has answers for each section, continue to part three.

Part three – have a feedback conversation

Ask your partner to give you their responses to each question in turn. Make sure that you understand each response, and use questions to clarify if necessary, e.g. 'Can you tell me a little more about that?' or 'Can you think of an example?' Receive all feedback graciously, maturely, and don't contradict the other person's view – after all, it's just their view. If they say something that you don't like or disagree with, simply find out a little more about what may have caused this view. When your partner has finished, thank them.

Part four – take the learning

Now, on your own, sit down with a piece of paper and write answers/notes to the following questions:

Q What did I learn about myself from that conversation?

Q What will I do differently as a result of that conversation?

Q What was not good about that conversation?

Q What am I going to do about that?

Q What was good about the way they gave me feedback?

Q What didn't work about the way they gave me feedback?

Q What principles will I focus on when giving feedback now?

Think also about how the conversation was useful to you generally. What was it like seeing yourself through the eyes of the other person?

Part five – share the learning (optional)

If you feel it is appropriate and useful, share your answers to the above questions with your partner. Ask them first if they'd like to hear them, as a way of sharing your learning. Remember, you'll now be in position of giving feedback yourself, so please employ all your learning and care!

Exercise summary **Giving supportive feedback**

As a coach, your observations and experience can make a significant difference to the person you're coaching. By making observations on the coachee's situation, the coach provides an external point of reference that the coachee can use to compare with their own thoughts and ideas.

When delivered with the appropriate balance of objective information and personal views, great feedback is a valuable contribution to the whole process of coaching.

General guidelines for giving feedback include:

➡ Know why you want to give feedback, i.e. your intent.

➡ Concentrate observation mostly on behaviour or facts.

➡ Balance objective and subjective statements wisely.

➡ Maintain the emotional state of the person you're giving feedback to, e.g. remain constructive.

Chapter summary **Fundamental skills of coaching**

The following skills are core to coaching, whether that's within a formal coaching session, or simply as a style of behaviour or management:

➡ Building rapport or relationship

➡ Different levels of listening

➡ Using intuition

➡ Asking questions

➡ Giving supportive feedback

These skills must be developed constantly, in order to keep them fresh and available. All of these skills are found in everyday situations, and you will already have a level of competence with each one. By exploring and practising aspects within each skill, we can develop our existing knowledge and ability, beyond what is normally found in an individual. When we are able to bring these skills together, coaching conversations flow naturally and easily.

Barriers to coaching

Often as important as what a good coach does is what a good coach doesn't do. There are a number of pitfalls even the most experienced coach might fall into that potentially impair the effectiveness of coaching. For example, the coach needs to maintain a level of influence in the conversation but must be careful not to control it. The coach must stay committed to the goals of the coachee but not become attached to them over time. In this chapter, we look at limiting behaviours or beliefs that obstruct effective coaching. By using the word barrier, we're simply looking at things that get in the way of good coaching practice.

Physical and environmental barriers

Some barriers include things relating to the coaching environment, e.g. is the room too hot/cold/noisy etc. Even lighting can distract a conversation – sit in a room with a flickering strip light and you'll know what I mean! I'm not going to go through all these physical or environmental barriers here, as I think they're either obvious or a matter of personal preference. For example, a coach will normally know what kind of environment they want to create, and also appreciate the amount of influence they have over that.

Is your room right?

The type of room you use can make a real difference to a coaching session. When I coach within business I have less control over where I'll be coaching than when I coach within my own premises. I'll request a private, quiet room of a reasonable size and location but I don't always get it! It's then up to my own judgement as to whether to attempt the coaching within that environment or not.

The following questions will help you to choose the right room for your coaching sessions.

Checklist **Is your room right for coaching?**

Q Is your room quiet enough?

Q Are the chairs in the room comfortable but not 'cosy'? (You want to stay awake.)

Q Is the room private, i.e. away from other people's hearing, out of view etc.?

Q Can you sit where you can see and hear your coachee properly?

Q Is your coachee happy and comfortable with the room?

As you can see, the above list requires a combination of common sense and practical thinking. However, the above are only guidelines, and a good coach can usually work effectively in very difficult conditions. The coach's personal preference and choice will ultimately determine whether they continue coaching in a particular environment or not.

Of course, coaching doesn't have to happen in a room. Other potentially wonderful environments can be found outdoors – in the forest, on a quiet, deserted beach, in a beautiful garden. The possibilities are endless and I encourage you to consider your options!

Fatigue

Some barriers relate simply to the state of the coach. Avoiding fatigue can become a problem, especially when coaching sessions are quite long or a coach is doing many different sessions in one day. Fatigue can cause a lack of concentration, poor retention/memory, lack of patience, inflexibility, etc.

The experience of dealing with a worn-out coach isn't great for the coachee either. The coachee may view the coach's low energy as disinterest, boredom or a simple inability to listen properly.

One solution obviously lies in scheduling a reasonable amount of sessions in one day, and allowing time between sessions to recuperate. For example, a coach might schedule four 1½ hour sessions, with 15 minutes between each session. In theory, this leaves the coach enough time to take a walk, grab a drink, and relax a little. In addition, the coach would schedule at least a 45-minute lunch break, to enable them to recuperate even more.

A problem arises when the session runs over time and through into the next one. This might be caused by different factors, some of which seem unavoidable. One such example can occur when it appears that a conversation will be cut short or impaired by being drawn to an unnatural close. Coaching conversations can ebb and flow like tides, and to call 'time' might go against this flow. Maybe the coachee is discussing something really important to them, or maybe the coach feels that a significant issue or break-through is just surfacing.

Another cause of delay might be that the coachee has kept something until the end of the session that they really want to talk about. In summing up, the coach might ask something like 'Are we done for today?' At which point the coachee brings something up. Maybe they were wondering whether to mention it and suddenly decided to do so.

As much as possible, a good coach will work at managing the session time effectively. Surprisingly, this is sometimes easier in short coaching sessions, e.g. 15 minutes, than long ones, e.g. 2 hours. In a short session, both parties are automatically focused on the time available. In longer sessions, it's easier to get lost in the conversation and allow time to disappear. One solution is to keep a clock or watch visible on the table, perhaps explaining at the beginning of the session the reason why it's there.

I find it's best to be open about checking the time during a session. At an appropriate moment, it's usually acceptable to say something like 'Let's just check how we're doing for time here.' That way, the coachee also becomes aware of the need to finish promptly.

Whatever the circumstances, the coach should do everything in their power to stay as resourceful as possible during the day. Simple things like drinking lots of water, taking regular breaks and eating the right foods help tremendously. I personally don't like to eat a large lunch during a day of coaching as I find I get tired and can't concentrate so well afterwards.

Anything that creates a sense of tiredness in the coach, e.g. lack of sleep, alcohol, etc. is best avoided.

Barriers relating to the coach's behaviour and belief

Less obvious and possibly more harmful to the coaching process are behaviours that the coach might adopt during coaching conversations that obstruct the collaborative coaching process. For example, asking too many questions for the coachee to respond to or displaying impatience when the coachee becomes confused or unclear. Again, practicality and common sense are needed to consider which behaviours work in coaching and which don't.

The behaviours we're going to explore can be both subtle and damaging to a collaborative coaching conversation. As with most principles we discuss in this book, there are no rights and no wrongs, only results or outcomes. For example, it's not wrong to ask too many questions, it's just unlikely to produce the results that the coach wants to produce.

So when we're coaching, we're looking to develop the following three-step process:

1   Become aware that we're doing or thinking something that's not working.

2   Acknowledge that – and give it up, i.e. let the thought go.

3   Substitute or re-focus with another more effective intention or behaviour.

I would also acknowledge that some of the following tendencies and behaviours might resonate with you more than others. For example, you may never find yourself trying to control or dominate others in conversation or talking too much. I would still encourage you to reflect on these barriers, as the more awareness of yourself you have, the better.

Too much talking

This may be another of those things that sound obvious for a coach not to do during a coaching conversation. It's actually quite easily done. Perhaps the coach is feeling particularly enthusiastic or energetic about a point they're making and 10 minutes later they are still talking. Alternatively, the coachee may seem reluctant to talk and so the coach fills the silent gaps by chatting.

In a collaborative coaching conversation, the coachee should be doing at least 70 per cent of the talking, often more. The principles of this type of coaching rest on the coachee being able to explore their own thoughts and experiences in such a way that evolves insight and learning. This simply isn't possible if they have to constantly listen to what the coach is saying.

Instead, a good coach uses a gentle process that involves them listening, asking questions, making observations or offering feedback. Occasionally the coach may choose to illustrate a point they are making by telling a short story, drawing a simple diagram – whatever is appropriate. Overall, the balance of all the talking will still rest with the coachee.

Less is more

Periods of quiet are often preferable to the irrelevant ramblings of a coach who has been embarrassed by silence. For the coachee, silence is often a good thing. By not having to speak or listen, the coachee can spend time in quiet reflection on their internal thought processes. Some thoughts and feelings take time to form, and further dialogue with the coach may distract or pressurize the coachee's internal thinking process.

For the coachee, silence is often a good thing.

A good coach will notice when the coachee appears to be reflecting on thoughts and ideas. Maybe the coach has just asked a question and the answer is not obvious, or maybe the coachee has just made an internal connection and wants to consider it a little. By allowing the room to fill with silence, the coach creates time and space for the coachee to simply think.

The following exercise will help you feel more comfortable about using silence.

An exercise **Just be quiet . . .**

Go and have a conversation with someone about something they are comfortable or familiar with. You might ask them about their weekend or something they're doing at work, anything that they can discuss easily. During the conversation, allow the conversation to fall silent if possible. For example, don't respond automatically when they pause in the conversation. Use one or two moments of silence as a way of deepening the conversation, or allowing them to speak again.

After the conversation, consider the following:

Q What effects did the silences have on the conversation?

Q During any silences how did you feel?

Q What opportunity does silence provide in a conversation?

Q When does using silence not work?

Emotional states

Generally, a coach wants to be in a resourceful state of mind and body to be able to coach to the best of their ability. As well as physical conditions such as general fatigue, or even illness, the coach must also be in a good emotional state to coach well.

Emotional states conducive to coaching include feeling relaxed, feeling aware, feeling focused, objective, even slightly detached. Emotional states unsupportive of coaching would include feeling angry, hostile, frustrated, impatient, anxious or simply bored.

Good coaches learn over time how to manage their own feelings and emotions within a coaching session. Different factors may challenge the coach's ability to do this, and the following may all happen to knock a coach off balance:

➡ The coaching session is interrupted by a fire alarm.

➡ You arrive for the session to find the room you wanted is double-booked.

➡ People keep walking into the meeting room you're in without knocking.

➡ You're coaching all day in the same room, it's freezing, and the drinks machine is broken.

➡ The coachee begins the session by saying they want to quit the coaching as it's not right for them.

To name but a few! As much as humanly possible, a coach must maintain a way of being within the sessions that enables effective coaching to happen. A coach's ability to listen, focus, ask the right questions and generally encourage progress depends on their emotional state. Whatever happens, they must respond resourcefully. For example, if the fire alarm goes off, leave the building in a relaxed manner and continue chatting if possible. If the room is double-booked, go and find another. If the coachee wants to quit, gently explore their reasons why (before jumping to conclusions).

I find that a combination of commitment and detachment really helps. For example, I can remind myself I'm committed to the success of the coaching and not attached as to how that might happen. Who knows? The fact that we have to break the session to walk out as part of a fire drill may be just the interruption we need to stimulate fresh conversation!

Sympathy as an emotional state

Within coaching, it's important that we understand the nature of both empathy and sympathy as they can create very different results.

Empathy means the ability to identify mentally with another person. In other words, if you feel sad, I can relate to that, and if you are angry, I can appreciate how you feel. Empathy does not mean that I feel what you feel, only that I can relate to how you feel.

The word sympathy means to share in an emotion or feeling with another person, so that two people experience similar emotional states at the same time. For example, if you feel sad, I am sad, and if you feel angry, so do I.

For example, a coachee is very angry or upset about something; maybe a work colleague has said something really cruel or unkind. Perhaps the coach sympathizes by also becoming angry and upset, 'Well that's awful, that makes me mad just to hear about it and I wasn't even there!' This is not a helpful view for the coach to take. The coach is becoming personally involved in the issue in a way that's not appropriate.

By sympathizing and becoming angry, the coach is also suggesting that they support the coachee's anger about the situation. Also, the coach should remain mostly objective about what they are hearing, in order to maintain a balanced perspective on situations. If the coach becomes angry or upset as well, rational thought is difficult.

In this instance, empathy would be a more effective way of responding to the coachee, e.g. 'You sound quite angry about that and I can appreciate why. Do you want to say more about what happened?' By acknowledging the coachee's anger whilst remaining fairly objective, the coach can continue to facilitate the conversation from a perspective of learning.

Additionally, a coach who continually sympathizes throughout coaching sessions is likely to become emotionally drained. Taking on the emotions of others is something that counsellors and therapists are trained to guard against or deal with because of the debilitating effects over time.

When empathy seems cold

There are times when empathy is not appropriate in relating to a coachee's emotion. Empathy is fine in response to more typical emotions of mild frustration, annoyance, disappointment etc. The risk of merely empathizing with the coachee is that sometimes this can appear a little cold and unsupportive.

Sometimes, situations and events demand a more sympathetic response. For example, a coachee has just experienced a significant loss of some sort and is visibly upset by it. For a coach to say 'I can appreciate how that must feel' might be inappropriate. To begin to objectively explore the situation, or look for possible learning, may not be what is needed right then. Maybe the coachee simply wants to know that their sadness is normal, and that the coach is genuinely caring in that moment. In this instance, sympathy often feels more caring to the individual, as the coach is demonstrating that they are willing to take on the experience of their sadness, e.g. 'Scott that's awful, I'm so sorry.' When the coach takes on the coachee's sadness, they obviously become more personally related to the coachee's situation.

This delicate balance rests on a combination of factors. The coach must consider what the coachee might want and what seems effective for the coaching at that point. The coach might also consider the potential impact on the ongoing coaching relationship. In addition, the coach needs to stay resourceful for the conversation and that isn't helped if they have sunk into a similar emotional state as the coachee.

Of course sometimes this level of restraint just isn't possible. Some things strike such a chord with the coach that they will genuinely be unable to control their response. That's human, natural and a real part of the coaching relationship.

Seeking to control or dominate the conversation

Collaborative coaching is based on encouraging the coachee to explore their own thoughts or experiences in a way that promotes insight and learning.

Collaborative coaching is based on encouraging the coachee to explore their own thoughts or experiences in a way that promotes insight and learning. If a coach controls the direction or content of a conversation in a way that inhibits its natural flow, then that's counterproductive.

It is important for the coach to maintain a balance between keeping the conversation focused and supporting its natural flow. The next example illustrates too much control by the coach:

COACH: 'So tell me more about the situation with your father. I want to find out exactly what the problem is and also what's causing his behaviour. I'm going to make sure we get to the bottom of this now.'

COACHEE: 'Well, what is it you want to know?'

COACH: 'Tell me about the most recent argument you've had with him and how he made you feel.'

As you can see from the dialogue, the coach is being both directive and authoritative during the conversation. In this case, the coachee adopts a compliant, almost submissive, posture, saying, 'Well, what is it you want to know?' This places the coach firmly in control of the direction and content of the conversation. The next thing they will discuss will be what the coach wants to discuss. There is much less space in the conversation for the natural flow of the conversation to emerge.

The next example demonstrates a coach maintaining a focus, whilst enabling the flow of the conversation to emerge and develop:

COACH: 'So tell me a little more about the situation with your father.'

COACHEE: 'Well, he's just being totally unsupportive of my efforts to get into college, he just keeps telling me to get out and get a job.'

COACH: 'What else does he say?'

COACHEE: 'He says I'm wasting my time, that I'm going to be disappointed, let down when I can't get the course that I want.'

COACH: 'What might be his reasons for saying that?'

COACHEE: 'I guess because he thinks I might do what my brother did when he was rejected. My brother ended up doing nothing for a year, just sat round the house being miserable.'

As you can see, the coach uses open questions to gently surface information from the coachee. If either party has the balance of control, it's probably the coachee. The coachee is causing the direction of the conversation to emerge based on the information they are offering.

Another subtle form of control is demonstrated in the following dialogue:

COACHEE: 'So I've decided that I'm not taking the job – they can keep it.'

COACH: 'Before you met the manager, didn't you say you wanted the job?'

COACHEE: 'Well, yes – but things have changed now.'

COACH: 'And didn't you say you wanted a challenge?'

COACHEE: 'Yes, I still do.'

COACHEE: 'Well, if you wanted the job and you wanted a challenge, isn't this the perfect opportunity for you?'

In this example, the coach is using a series of tactically worded questions to close down the options of the coachee. The questions are closed questions (only yes or no responses are possible), leaving the coachee little room to explain themselves properly. The coach is adopting an inappropriate level of control over the conversation. As a result, the coachee's own thoughts and insights cannot be expressed fully and the full potential of the situation is unlikely to emerge.

This subtle form of control also places the coach in a superior position to the coachee. Rather like a cat toying with a mouse, the coach is adopting a position of intellectual superiority to the coachee.

A more collaborative version of the previous dialogue might be:

COACHEE: 'So I've decided that I'm not taking the job – they can keep it.'

COACH: 'Okay, can you tell me a little more about that?'

COACHEE: 'Well, I don't seem to be what they're looking for I guess.'

COACH: 'What are they looking for do you think?'

COACHEE: 'Well, they seem to want someone energized and motivated, I've felt so low for so long in my current job I've forgotten what that's like.'

As you can see, the conversation goes in a completely different direction once the coach adopts a more open style of questioning. So what might cause a coach to try and control the conversation? The following are all possible factors:

➡ The coach thinks they've spotted a solution to a problem and wants to lead the coachee towards it.

→ The coach is frustrated at the amount of time it's taking to discuss a subject.

→ The coach thinks the coachee expects them to take control.

→ The coachee seems unwilling to discuss an area, and the coach really wants them to.

→ The coachee has high energy or enthusiasm for the topic under discussion.

→ The coach knows a lot about the subject being discussed and wants to display this knowledge.

→ The coach has a naturally authoritative manner in conversation and is used to 'leading from the front', e.g. they have a very 'strong' personality, maybe they're a senior manager, etc.

Again, awareness is the key to choice. By noticing when we're controlling the content and direction of a conversation, we can reduce this influence immediately. Our efforts and energy need to go into listening and facilitating thoughts, rather than constructing the conversation. In doing so, we open up the potential for a natural flow of thoughts and ideas to emerge.

An exercise **Letting go of control**

The following exercises will help you give up control during a conversation:

➡ Help someone else find the answer (pp. 49–51)

➡ Developing deep listening (pp. 138–40)

Needing to be 'right'

We like being right and we don't enjoy being wrong. Some of us are better at finding out we're wrong than others. (Some of us are really lousy at being wrong!) In coaching, I would recommend that any coach give up an attachment to being right – it simply gets in the way of the conversation.

An attachment to being right is closely linked to our need to look good in conversations. In order to let go of an attachment to being right, we must also give up an attachment to looking good.

For example, a coachee may be discussing setting up home with a new partner, and complaining that they are having second thoughts. The coach may have a theory about why this is and become inadvertently attached to it, as follows:

COACH: 'Well, I think the reason you're having doubts is because you're anticipating everything that could go wrong. After all, it's a big step for you.'

COACHEE: 'No, it's not that, I haven't actually thought about what could go wrong.'

COACH: 'Yes, but a lot of these things happen subconsciously. I think you're experiencing transference – that means you're transferring the real problem in order to disguise it.'

In this example, the coach has made several mistakes. Firstly, they've played a subtle form of 'fix-it,' by seeking to come up with a reason for the coachee's misgivings. It might have been more effective to explore the situation more fully before making any observation.

Secondly, they've become attached to proving that their theory is right. Because of this attachment, they are influencing the conversation in a direction that is inappropriate. The conversation might easily develop into looking for things the coachee thinks might go wrong, or even why they haven't been thinking about what might go wrong.

If a coach makes a mistake or gets something wrong, they should deal with it in a mature, unattached way.

Finally, the coach seems to have slipped into the behaviour of looking good. By using words like 'transference' the coach is displaying their knowledge of psychology. The effect on the coachee is likely to be one of confusion and/or defensiveness.

If a coach makes a mistake or gets something wrong, they should deal with it in a mature, unattached way. There's a simple three-step approach that I use:

1 Acknowledge I'm wrong, either to myself or the coachee (whatever is appropriate).

2 Put the mistake right if possible/appropriate.

3 Give up thoughts of being wrong – move on.

For example, to repeat the previous example in a more effective way:

COACH: 'Well, I think the reason you're having doubts is because you're anticipating everything that could go wrong. After all, it's a big step for you.'

COACHEE: 'No, it's not that, I haven't actually thought about what could go wrong.'

COACH: 'Okay, that's probably me jumping to conclusions. Tell me more about what you've been thinking.'

Very quickly, and smoothly, the coach acknowledges the error and continues the coaching conversation. Both the coach and the coachee can carry on with the natural flow of the conversation uninterrupted.

Within coaching, it's okay to make mistakes and get things wrong. All coaches do. What's not okay is for a coach to spend time and effort justifying or disguising errors or mistakes. To do so may confuse, disrupt or impair the coaching process.

Playing 'fix-it'

When a coach plays 'fix-it' they assume that the coachee has a problem and it's up to them as coach to find the answer. The coach will focus their efforts on searching for a problem in what's being said and then trying to solve it. The drawbacks of this include:

➡ The coach develops an inappropriate filter to listen only for problems.

➡ The coach tries to come up with solutions without the input of the coachee.

➡ The coachee can end up feeling flawed or inadequate – something of a 'problem case'.

Watch the following dialogue for signs of the coach playing fix-it:

COACHEE: 'So really, I don't know why I've taken on organizing the party at all. It's typical of me to get stuck with something like this.'

COACH: 'Well, why don't you cancel it?'

COACHEE: 'Oh I couldn't do that, we'd lose money on caterers and flowers and things.'

COACH: 'Can you get someone else to help you, then?'

COACHEE: 'Not at this late stage, and besides, why should I ask – they should be offering!'

COACH: 'Could you move the date, then?'

From the dialogue, the coach thinks that they have found the problem – namely that the coachee doesn't want to organize the party. Because the coach is playing 'fix-it', the coach is then reacting to incomplete information, guessing at possible solutions.

The coach needs to spend more time seeking to understand the situation, and let the conversation develop naturally. The next example demonstrates a better approach:

COACHEE: 'So really, I don't know why I've taken on organizing the party at all. It's typical of me to get stuck with something like this.'

COACH: 'Okay, can you tell me a little more about that?'

COACHEE: 'Well, I seem to be the one who ends up doing all the work. I wouldn't mind if anyone actually acknowledged me for it. A simple thanks would do.'

As you can see, the conversation has gone in a completely different direction, as the coach gently explores the situation. The 'problem' (if there is one) may turn out to be entirely different from initial impressions. Maybe the coachee simply wants to be acknowledged for their efforts, or for efforts they've made in the past.

By ignoring any temptation to find a problem and solve it, the coach helps both understanding and resolution emerge more naturally.

An exercise Stop playing 'fix-it'!

The following exercises will help you stop playing 'fix-it':

➡ Help someone else find the answer (pp. 49–51)

➡ Developing deep listening (pp. 138–40)

Assuming your experience is relevant

This trap is an easy one to fall into. When a coach does a lot of coaching, sometimes what the coachee is saying sounds just like something other coachees have discussed in the past – a sort of flawed version of déjà vu. Because the coach thinks the conversation or the situation is the same, they also expect other aspects of it to be the same as well. This might cause the coach to assume other facts around the situation to be the same, and the same solution or way forward to be of benefit.

For example, a coachee is describing problems with their boss at work. The coachee says that their boss interferes too much in their work and this is causing them frustration and annoyance. The coach is listening to the coachee and an internal voice says, 'Aha, this sounds familiar, this is just like that other situation – it's all about lack of understanding of the boss's intentions.'

From this thought, the coach can easily begin to jump to conclusions, e.g. that they totally understand the situation, or they know what will work as a way forward.

When coaching I'm mindful that what worked yesterday won't necessarily work today. Whatever totally brilliant insight, question or idea we had in a previous session, it could easily be irrelevant or inappropriate in my next one.

Staying focused

The other pitfall of assuming relevant knowledge or experience in this way relates to the coach's focus or attention. Once again, if the coach diverts their thoughts to recalling past coaching conversations, they might easily spend time drifting off thinking about previous events and lose focus on the present. In this way, the quality of the coach's attention and listening is impaired. This in turn affects their ability to appreciate fully what the coachee is telling them, and so coach effectively.

Looking for the 'perfect solution'

Sometimes in coaching we experience a magical 'Aha!' moment between the coach and the coachee. A fabulous idea or insight presents itself and the perfect way forward for the coachee appears. Problems dissolve, blockages are cleared and the sun comes out. For a coach, this feels great. They know that by the process of their conversation they have really made a difference to the coachee. The 'buzz' of the whole experience can be quite uplifting for the coach and also mildly addictive.

The issue with this arises when the coach attempts to repeat it in subsequent coaching sessions. The coach assumes that there's a wonderful solution to every coachee's situation and attempts to find one in each session. In this way, the coach is guaranteed obvious results in the form of amazing breakthroughs and ideas. Also, the coach will regularly experience the 'high' of that wonderful moment when the magical solution or insight is found.

Personal coaching is usually an ongoing process, where insights and learning can emerge as much between coaching sessions as they do in them.

In reality, these moments are fairly rare in coaching, and usually occur when a coach least expects them. Certainly trying to produce them rarely works. Personal coaching is usually an ongoing process, where insights and learning can emerge as much between coaching sessions as they do in them. For a coach to try always to produce fast or amazing results can distort their view of the conversation.

Ultimately, the coachee determines the value and effectiveness of coaching. Some coachees don't need amazing insights or breakthroughs. They simply need support with their learning and development processes.

Perfection is in the eye of the beholder

Sometimes the perfect solution for the coachee doesn't look perfect to the coach. For example, a coachee is describing how his studies at night school are interfering with his social life. The course that he's taken falls on the same night as his bowling club's match nights.

During the process of the coaching conversation the coachee realizes that if he leaves the evening class 30 minutes early, he can still make the bowling evening. At this point, the coachee seems pleased he's found what feels like a workable compromise. The coach doesn't think that this sounds like a perfect solution. After all, the nursing qualification he's taking is really important to his life goals.

At this point, the coach has three options: (a) Accept the coachee's choice of a way forward; (b) Explore the potential risks and benefits of this option further; or (c) Encourage the coachee to think of something else.

If the coach is still looking for the 'perfect' solution, they will pursue option (c) and continue looking for another idea. This may cause the coachee to feel uncomfortable as what feels to him to be a great idea is being disregarded.

If the coach genuinely feels that this is a flawed idea but simply accepts it anyway (option (a)), then they risk sharing the burden of the ultimate consequences. Maybe the coachee's class work suffers, and so he doesn't get that qualification that was so important to him.

Bad ideas usually expose themselves very quickly when they are explored more fully. Likewise, apparently flawed ideas expose themselves as perfect by the same process of exploration. The following dialogue illustrates this principle, as the coach takes option (b) and explores the potential risks and benefits of the idea:

COACH: 'How will leaving the class early affect your studies?'

COACHEE: 'Oh, not at all. The last half-hour is always a reading time. I can do that on the bus ride home.'

COACH: 'And what will your tutor say if you request to leave early?'

COACHEE: 'Well, if I'm doing the reading I don't think she'll mind. She's very easy-going as long as we keep up with our homework, which I always do.'

So ultimately, the coachee's idea appears workable. It may still not seem perfect to the coach, certainly not enough to produce lightning bolts or cries of 'Eureka!' The point is if the coach persists in pursuing a perfect solution, it may easily become a frustrating and pointless process for both parties. They may easily end up back where they started, with the coachee's first idea being the only practical way forward.

Trying to look good in the conversation

As humans, we have a need to look good in the eyes of other people and ourselves. In coaching, this can get in the way of an effective conversation. It gets in the way because it diverts the coach's attention from staying fully present in the conversation. When the coach is not fully present, the following can be true:

⮕ The coach's mind can be focused too much on themselves, and not enough on the coachee.

⮕ The coach is not as truthful, open and honest as they could be.

⮕ Because the coach is not as open and honest, they are less powerful in the conversation.

By 'looking good', I refer to our almost subconscious tendency to maintain an appearance that we feel is in some way positive. When a coach devotes effort or energy to looking good in the conversation, it detracts from the quality of their attention and the effectiveness of their coaching. A coach may do or say things in order to impress, rather than for the actual benefit of the coaching conversation.

This probably relates to the ego, our sense of self or self-consciousness and some instinctive reluctance ever to seem vulnerable to others. Whatever causes it, I hope you'll have fun recognizing it in yourself and your own behaviour – as I do.

Within coaching, there are various pressures upon the coach to 'look good'. Where a coach is delivering the service of coaching, it follows that the coachee may have certain expectations of them, for example, that the coach appears to:

⮕ Have all the answers.

⮕ Say clever or smart things.

⮕ Have a real impact.

⮕ Be professional, businesslike.

⮕ Be very experienced/knowledgeable.

⮕ Know just what to say within the conversation.

⮕ Have a happy, fulfilling life free of problems or conflict.

Wanting to look good isn't a 'bad' thing; it's a way we've learned to cope with some of the risks and pressures of life. We might assume that the alternative to 'looking good' is 'looking bad' – and that feels wrong to us. Actually, the alternative to using behaviours intended to make us 'look good' is simply to be our natural selves.

For example, a coachee is saying how they'd really like to exercise more but they just don't feel like it. The coach just happens to have studied various theories of human motivation. So the coach spends the next 15 minutes describing Maslow's hierarchy of needs and drawing diagrams on paper as proof of this knowledge. The coach forgets the original point which led to the discussion of this theory, as they are enjoying demonstrating how much they know. In the meantime, the coachee has become bored with the conversation and doesn't see how it relates to why he can't be bothered to go to the gym anymore.

The coach has fallen into the trap of wanting to appear knowledgeable to the coachee. This may be in order to gain more credibility, or simply because they enjoy appearing knowledgeable. Unfortunately the coach effectively diverted the conversation from something important and relevant – which was the coachee's lack of motivation. Instead they focused the conversation to something less relevant, i.e. a lengthy, theoretical explanation of Maslow's hierarchy of needs. If we'd interrupted the coach part-way through his explanation and asked him 'Why are you saying this stuff now?', a really truthful answer would be 'because I think it's impressive/sounds good . . .'

Staying present in the conversation

Any time we increase our awareness of ourselves, our appearance, how we're sounding, etc., we decrease our awareness of the other person. We become 'not present' to the person and to what's happening in the conversation. As a result, our quality of listening diminishes, and our ability to notice non-verbal signals from the coachee is impaired. Literally, we become less conscious.

Staying present to what's happening requires commitment and concentration. Our reward within coaching conversations is better understanding and a sense of relatedness. The following exercise will help you practise.

An exercise Are you present?

Overview

In conversation, we focus quite a lot on our own thoughts, what's being said, what we're thinking of saying, etc. This exercise demands that we let those thoughts go, as we focus solely on what's really happening. This can be a real challenge and also incredibly rewarding!

Step one – on your own

Becoming present requires us to refocus our attention into the here and now. Do it now. Lift your head up from reading this and focus on wherever you are – your surroundings. What can you see and what can you hear? Let your mind go quiet, as you become acutely aware of what's actually going on.

Step two – with someone else

Go and have a conversation with someone, and practise being 'present' whilst you're talking to them. Really focus your attention on them and what they're saying. The more you get present with them, the more your mind will go quiet as you begin to notice them properly. Any time your mind drifts off, wanders, starts thinking of something else, simply bring it back to what's happening there and then. When you speak, get really present to what you're saying, experience your own words, and the impact they have.

Step three – focus on learning

After the conversation, ask yourself the following questions:

Q What was different about the conversation when you remained present?

Q What did you have to do to become present?

Q If you remained present more in your future conversations, what impact would that have?

Confusion can be powerful

Another form of the 'looking good' trap arises from the gentle expectation from the coachee that the coach has all the answers and will always know the perfect thing to say. Sometimes, the most authentic and powerful thing a coach can do is to acknowledge that they are as confused by a situation as the coachee. At least then they can work through the facts and issues together. For the coach to pretend they understand, or take a wild guess at what might be an answer may take the conversation in a wholly inappropriate direction.

Strategizing in the conversation

Another barrier to effective coaching is a subtle form of control known as strategizing. Strategizing is what happens when the coach starts saying or doing things in order to create a certain outcome. For example, a coach may say something in order to provoke a reaction or deliberately take an opposing view. Here, the coach might reason that they had good intentions for playing these mental forms of chess with the coachee. Whatever the coach's reasons for doing it – they were still strategizing.

There are many ways a coach might strategize in a coaching conversation, and they all have one thing in common. When a coach is strategizing, they are saying what they are saying 'in order to get a certain result' and they prefer this motive to remain concealed from the coachee.

That might be to get the coachee to do or say a certain thing, in order to get them to see something a certain way, feel a certain way, etc. There's a subtle note of covert manipulation to strategizing that enables us to distinguish it from anything else.

For example, maybe a coach is thinking, 'This conversation just isn't working, and I don't know why.' The coach might feel uncomfortable about voicing that and so decides to take another route to explore the issue. So the coach says, 'Let's look at our original goals here.' This may or may not address the underlying issue (that the coach doesn't think the conversation is 'working').

If the coach were being more truthful, they would say, 'I keep thinking that this conversation isn't working – can we explore that a little?' This is likely to open up a conversation that exposes what's happening. If the conversation isn't working for the coach, it probably isn't for the coachee either. By approaching the subject openly and directly, the coach can explore what's really happening. Maybe the coachee wants to talk about something completely different, and has been preoccupied with that from the beginning of the session. If the coach hides what they are thinking, and asks, 'Let's look at our original objectives here', the coachee's preoccupation is unlikely to surface. By strategizing, the coach has avoided tackling the issue directly.

Being authentic – speaking our truth

The opposite of strategizing is being authentic. When we are authentic, we speak our truth, we say what's there, and this is not corrupted or changed in any way. For example, if we're worried about driving on the motorway we declare, 'I'm worried about driving on the motorway.' We do not say, 'Let's go the country route, it's prettier.' In coaching, this level of honesty is needed to create openness and trust within the coaching relationship. It's also a more powerful way to communicate.

If the coach is busy strategizing, they are not fully present with the coachee and are not being authentic in their views.

If the coach is busy strategizing, they are not fully present with the coachee and are not being authentic in their views. The mental effort of translating one thought into different words diverts energy from being with the coachee and developing the conversation naturally. It's almost as if the coach is having two conversations, one with themselves, and another with the coachee.

Example of strategizing

COACHEE:	'Well, I just don't agree with the feedback forms from my colleagues, how can they say I withhold information?' 'I think we should disregard those comments as malicious rubbish.'
COACH THINKS:	[I've heard you say 'information is power in this place' repeatedly and also that you don't tell anyone anything that they don't need to know.]

COACH SAYS:	(in order to avoid giving more difficult feedback) 'What might have caused these comments, do you think?'
COACHEE:	'No idea. Some people just don't like to see others getting on, I guess.'

The coach is effectively hiding what they are thinking. This may be to protect the coachee from a potentially hurtful thought, or even avoid a confrontation. Unfortunately, this may not create much learning for the coachee. One of the core coaching skills is the ability to give challenging messages in a constructive way, as supportive feedback. This skill enables the coach to say what needs to be said, in order to progress the coachee's awareness.

Example of being authentic

COACHEE:	'Well, I just don't agree with the feedback forms from my colleagues, how can they say I withhold information?' 'I think we should disregard those comments as malicious rubbish.'
COACH THINKS:	[I've heard you say 'information is power in this place' repeatedly and also that you don't tell anyone anything that they don't need to know.]
COACH SAYS:	'That's quite a tough message, isn't it? And as I hear it, I can see potential links to some comments you made in the last session – can I offer you those?'
COACHEE:	'Sure – I'd love to know what's going on here!'
COACH SAYS:	'When we were discussing the management team meetings, you said you reported the minimum of your department's plans as "knowledge is power in this place". And when we talked more about that you said you saw no reason to tell anyone anything that they didn't need to know. I'm just wondering if we aren't seeing some of the effects of that here.'
COACHEE:	'Yes, but everyone does that, don't they?'

COACH SAYS:	'I don't know, and right now what's important to me is you, and what works for you. Right now it seems like this approach to reporting information might not be working for you.'
COACHEE:	'Well, I'm beginning to see that now – silly isn't it? You think you're playing by the rules and it turns out you're not!'

Giving up strategizing

The way to avoid strategizing begins with catching ourselves doing it. We need to develop an internal alarm bell for this behaviour. When coaching, if I notice I'm saying something in order to produce a result that I've predicted, mine goes off! For example, I might decide I know 'the answer' to the situation. Then all I have to do is get the coachee to see this answer.

The trouble is, as soon as I start doing this I begin strategizing. Using the previous example, maybe I think that it's a good idea to talk to the person hiring their job about their concerns. I then start to ask a series of questions to lead them to that conclusion. Now, I may or may not be right with my idea. The point is that strategizing with it can lead me into trouble. It is actually far more honest, and usually effective, simply to declare my own thoughts at that point, e.g. 'I keep thinking about the option of speaking to the person hiring the job about your concerns. What do you think?'

Another place to practise giving up strategizing is in normal everyday conversation. Wherever we have an agenda for a conversation, or think we know how it's going to go, we tend to strategize. Have a go, especially in conversations with people you're a little wary of, and observe how we make 'moves' in conversation, rather like intellectual chess!

A simple example: your partner wants to go out for dinner tonight and you're too tired. You don't want to say so, because you think that sounds lame. So instead you start asking questions to change your partner's mind, e.g. 'Won't it be difficult to get a booking?', 'Aren't we supposed to be saving money?' or 'Who's going to drive and not drink?'

Once you have noticed yourself doing it, you can give it up. You might choose to declare your hidden thought or feeling, or simply let it go. Maybe a good night out is just what you need to refresh your spirits!

An exercise | Where are you strategizing?

The following exercise is intended to help you develop your own awareness of when you might be strategizing. In addition, it will also help you speak your own thoughts more authentically.

You will be using a conversation with someone to notice the difference between what you think, and what you actually say. Pick a conversation with someone who you aren't very close to, perhaps you're less relaxed in their company, or just never became really familiar with them. A work colleague might work well – a partner or best friend might not.

Step one – develop awareness

During the conversation, develop an awareness of that moment just before you say something. Maybe the other person has just said something to you and you're going to respond to their statement or question. At that moment, you might first have a thought, maybe an opinion – do you respond with that thought? How much difference is there between what you're thinking, and what you're actually saying?

Step two – practise authentic responses (optional)

Where you notice a difference between your true (authentic) thought or view, and the response you might normally give, instead give a response that more accurately reflects your views. This will feel like you are speaking your own truth, rather than what you think might sound 'right' or appropriate. It's probably easier to begin with something minor, like a true response to the question 'How are you?' or 'How did you like that film?' So say what you really think, rather than what you think might be expected.

Step three – focus on learning

After the conversation, consider the following:

Q How much did your speech match your real thoughts and views?

Q What causes the difference in what you thought from what you said?

Q How does speaking your real thoughts and views feel?

Q What would happen if you matched your thoughts to your speech more often?

Q When might this not work very well?

Exercise summary **Where are you strategizing?**

This exercise is simply to draw our attention to times we might be strategizing, and that's not always easy is it? When you're feeling more comfortable, you might choose other conversations to speak your truth more powerfully on more significant matters. For example, what you think about a difficult situation or perhaps a decision that's being made.

Focusing on what not to do

So now that we've discussed several things a coach needs 'not' to do during coaching sessions, I've created another. There's an obvious risk in focusing on what not to do during a coaching conversation. For example, if I tell you *not to think about* a blue rabbit wearing sunglasses, what do you think about? (Surely not a blue rabbit wearing sunglasses!)

So a coach needs to not think about what they are not supposed to be doing . . . confused? That's exactly the point.

If a coach's head is full of thoughts like 'Don't control the conversation, don't treat them like they're a problem, don't take on their feelings too much,' obviously that's not going to work. The coach's head is then full of their own internal conversation rather than listening to the coachee. In addition, by focusing on what not to do, they may easily end up doing it. Did you ever talk about a sensitive issue and say to yourself, 'Don't say the word failure' – then find that the word failure is the only word you can think of?

Within coaching the three-step process of awareness, acknowledgement and substitution can help to refocus thought.

Chapter summary **Barriers to coaching**

Much of the skill of coaching lies in what a good coach doesn't do, as well as what they do. Some behaviour is counterproductive to the coaching process, and simply gets in the way of a great conversation. Some of these are simple behaviours, like talking too much, whilst others relate to the coach's belief, e.g. a need to be right, or find the 'perfect solution'.

Once we become aware of these behavioural barriers, we are able to let them go. This follows a three-step process:

1 To become aware that we're doing or thinking something that's not working.

2 Acknowledge that – and give it up, i.e. let the thought go.

3 Substitute or refocus with another more effective intention or behaviour.

So key to avoiding these barriers to effective coaching is an ability to develop an intuitive sense of when we're doing them. As I've mentioned before, this begins with awareness. This includes awareness of the pitfalls, which potentially begins by you reading this. Then develop this awareness by consciously noticing your own tendencies to adopt these behaviours. First, create a focus for just one of them, e.g. playing fix-it, in your next conversation with someone who appears to have a problem. Make it a game to catch yourself doing it, then decide to give up doing it.

Over time, you won't have to wonder if you're doing it, as your subconscious will let you know. Intuitively, you may get a feeling or thought that you're not comfortable with the conversation. If you attend to that thought, you'll probably notice what it is that you're doing. At that point, simply acknowledge the realization, give up doing whatever you're doing, and move on, letting the thought go.

The power of substitution

One way for a coach to let go of a thought is to replace it with another thought in order to refocus their mind. For example, if a coach notices herself playing fix-it, she might remind herself, 'Just let the solutions emerge.' Alternatively, if the coach notices that they are talking too much in the conversation, they might silently say, 'listen and focus back on them.'

It's rather like noticing that you've got a lamp shining on the wrong side of a room. By moving the light you illuminate the appropriate area, whilst returning the other side to darkness.

chapter

7

Summary and close

Key points of learning

Collaborative coaching is an effective, respectful approach

Collaborative coaching is effective because of the underlying principles that support it, namely:

➡ The coachee experiences being truly listened to and appreciates the effort the coach makes to understand them.

➡ The relationship is based on equality, encouraging openness and trust. The coach is not claiming to have all the answers and the coachee feels their contribution is worthwhile.

➡ Insights, perspectives and ideas are highly relevant to the coachee, and they relate to them with both ownership and responsibility.

➡ As most ideas and actions come from the coachee, so does the responsibility for their action and results.

➡ Solutions are developed according to the understanding of the person experiencing the situation so they are normally of much higher relevance and effectiveness.

➡ Thoughts and ideas provoke ongoing learning in the mind of the coachee. As if the conversation is a pebble being thrown into a pond, questions are the catalyst that begins a reaction.

➡ If an idea doesn't get the result the coachee wanted, the coachee still feels ownership of the idea, and so will be more willing to work to get a better result.

By adopting a less directive style of conversation we focus much more on the internal learning processes of the coachee. We respectfully maintain the responsibility of the coachee for their situations, and retain a sense of equality within the coaching relationship.

A good coach can be defined by the principles they operate from as much as what they actually do

The principles a coach operates from create a foundation for everything they do. The following are key within a collaborative coaching approach:

➡ Maintain a commitment to support the individual.

➡ Build the coaching relationship on truth, openness and trust.

➡ The coachee is responsible for the results they are generating.

➡ The coachee is capable of much better results than they are currently generating.

➡ Focus on what the coachee thinks and experiences.

➡ Coachees can generate perfect solutions.

➡ The conversation is based on equality.

Use of these principles can sometimes have more impact than technical skill. For example, operating with a commitment to openness, honesty and trust can often do more for the coaching relationship than conscious rapport-building techniques.

Thinking about structure and process helps make coaching effective

An ongoing coaching relationship is made more effective by planning and preparation. By considering the key stages or components of the coaching process we are able to balance the amount of time we spend on these activities. These stages are highlighted again in Fig. 7.1.

It makes sense to consider these stages in the logical order they are indicated. That's not necessarily how they will occur, though, and the sequence of activities may need to be changed. Once these stages have begun, they become themes that are developed throughout the coaching. For example, once we've defined initial goals and a sense of direction for the assignment, we must maintain these over time.

Core skills can be identified and developed

The skills and disciplines needed to be a successful coach do not come naturally to most of us. Instead, they are ways of creating coaching conversations that we learn and develop constantly. The core skills of a collaborative coach are highlighted again in Fig. 7.2.

Fig. 7.1 Framework for a coaching assignment

Fig. 7.2 Fundamental coaching skills

Some coaches have some of these skills naturally, either because of their basic personality, or as a result of previous experiences and learning. Some skills require more technical competence, such as asking questions, and gaining these skills requires a more focused disciplined approach. Once acquired, these skills must be practised. Many everyday situations present opportunities to develop or maintain these skills, e.g. everyday conversations with colleagues or friends.

What a coach doesn't do is often as important as what they do

Certain behaviours or principles of behaviour form barriers to the development and flow of great coaching conversation. They include:

➡ Talking too much.

➡ Too much sympathy.

➡ Seeking to control or dominate the conversation

➡ Needing to be 'right'.

➡ Playing 'fix-it'.

➡ Assuming your experience is relevant.

➡ Looking for the 'perfect solution'.

➡ Trying to look good in the conversation.

➡ Strategizing in the conversation.

➡ Focusing on what not to do.

Some of these behaviours are simple traps to fall into, for any coach, no matter how experienced they are. Many arise from natural human tendencies such as being enthusiastic or enjoying solving other people's problems. So when we're coaching, we're looking to develop the following three-step process:

1 Become aware that we're doing or thinking something that's not working.

2 Acknowledge that – and give it up, i.e. let the thought go.

3 Substitute or refocus with another more effective intention or behaviour.

The future of coaching

Personal coaching as a field of human activity has grown significantly during the last 20 – and it continues to grow. No longer do we think of coaches as being associated only with the field of sports. We've got coaches in business, life coaches, coaching for presidents and politicians – wherever people strive to attain success and fulfilment, coaches are often at work.

So, the field of coaching is firmly established and is growing. It now needs to become more clearly defined. Too much of what constitutes coaching practices and approach remains a mystery to both client and coaches alike. Where a lack of clear definition exists, coaches waste valuable time and take unnecessary risks with coachees, trying to learn for themselves what works and what doesn't.

Great coaching can be transformational, causing dramatic improvements in both professional and personal situations.

Clients need to know what to look for when securing the services of a good coach. They need to know what to expect and what constitutes good coaching practice. They need to feel that their investments of time, effort and money constitute resources well spent. Great coaching can literally be transformational, causing dramatic improvements in both professional and personal situations. Poor quality coaching does no one any good, least of all the coaching profession itself.

Anyone interested in coaching as an activity or profession needs clear guidelines and principles to operate from. Coaches need the support of structure, process, tools and techniques upon which they can build a really great coaching practice.

Taking your learning forward

The person who ultimately benefits most from your learning and development as a coach is you. The skills gained within coaching – of awareness, communication, analysis and insight – are incredibly fulfilling. They're also invaluable life skills and help all of us in our own situations and relationships.

As a profession or simply as part of what you already do, coaching offers you an opportunity to make a real contribution to others. Good coaches can make a great difference. And no matter how experienced or skilled a coach is, there's always more to learn. New approaches, techniques and perspectives constantly emerge that keep us fresh and aware of the options available to us. So I hope this book has added to your own learning (I know it's added to mine). I encourage you to stay committed to your own self-development, and I wish you both enjoyment and success with that.

Closing summary

Coaching is ultimately a journey of discovery for both the coach and the coachee. In coaching, I'm sometimes profoundly affected by the conversation I've just had. Either I've had insights that were relevant to me, or I've simply been touched by what has occurred. Whilst it is never the purpose of the conversation, a coach can sometimes benefit from the coaching as much as the coachee.

So coaching is no ordinary work but a labour of love, often demanding, sometimes frustrating – always worthwhile. And if you accept the challenge of coaching, it's a lifelong journey of learning, where you'll experience the circle of giving and receiving constantly. Which makes me wonder – have you already accepted this challenge?

Further resources

For a recommended reading list, useful websites, course details and other resources, see www.business-minds.com/goto/coachingmanual.

Appendix 1

Coaching overview document

What is this?	➡ An overview of coaching.
What does it do?	➡ Gives someone an initial understanding of coaching, what it is, possible benefits, etc.
	➡ Encourages a coachee to begin thinking about any goals or objectives they might have.
When might I use it?	➡ During initial discussions about the potential of coaching.
	➡ When beginning a new coaching relationship, to give a new coachee some background information or reading.

Introduction

A coaching overview document is intended to:

➡ Give an overview of personal coaching, what it is, how it works, and its potential benefits.

➡ Describe what you can expect from your coach, and what your coach will expect from you.

➡ Encourage you to think about how coaching might benefit you.

What is personal coaching?

Coaching is a form of learning, where a person – a coach – supports someone else – a coachee – to create learning and self-development in a way that benefits them.

From early forms of transportation, i.e. stagecoach, or rail coach, the word 'coaching' literally means to transport someone from one place to another. One thing that all forms of coaching seem to have in common is that people are using it to help them move forward in a certain direction.

One simple example is probably that of a sports coach. Here, the coach supports the individual to improve their performance and get better results – depending on what they want to achieve. For a golfer, the goal might be winning a major tournament, or simply improving their grip. The role of the coach is to apply specific principles of success, in a way that creates experiential learning and improvement for the golfer.

Coaching is normally a conversation, or series of conversations, one person has with another. The coach intends to produce a conversation that will benefit the other person, the coachee, in a way that relates to the coachee's learning and progress. Coaching conversations might happen in many different ways, and in many different environments.

For example, coaching might consist of two people talking in a room about things the coachee wants to change. This is sometimes called 'off-line' coaching. It might also be one person observing another person doing something, e.g. chairing a meeting, then discussing that afterwards. This can be called on-line coaching.

Why do people have coaching?

People enlist the services of a coach because they want to improve their situations and achieve goals. They want to learn new ways of thinking and approaching situations, in order to get better results. Common goals might be being more organized and effective at work, gaining confidence in certain situations, or simply relating to other people more effectively.

A skilled coach uses a combination of observation, questioning, listening and feedback to create a conversation rich in insight and learning. For the coachee, they will experience a focus and attention that enable them to develop a greater awareness and appreciation of their own circumstances. In addition, they'll also create new ways to resolve issues, produce better results and generally achieve their goals more easily.

Common benefits people experience from coaching include:

➡ Improved sense of direction and focus.

➡ Increased knowledge of self/self-awareness.

➡ Improved ability to relate to and influence others.

➡ Increased motivation.

➡ Improved personal effectiveness, e.g. focused effort.

➡ Increased resourcefulness/resilience, e.g. ability to handle change.

What coaching is not

Coaching is none of the following.

Structured training, e.g. classroom learning

Structured training relates to a fixed agenda of learning, and a prepared approach to making that learning happen. For example, if you were being trained in a classroom to use a computer, the trainer would often use a structured approach to making sure you learnt a certain amount of information, within a certain time frame.

Coaching follows a more flexible format, according to the coachee's objectives. Both the coachee and the coach influence the direction and content of sessions. Coaching also places real responsibility for learning on the individual and encourages learning to continue after the session.

Therapy, psychoanalysis, psychotherapy

Whilst coaching is not therapy, and should not be viewed as therapy, it does provide a viable alternative to people who may have previously considered some form of counselling to resolve a situation. For example, coaching promotes a greater self-awareness, and fuller appreciation of our own situations and circumstances. Sometimes, change can be promoted by a simple shift in perspectives. Barriers of self-belief such as 'I can't' or 'I don't' can be challenged in order to encourage fresh approaches and ideas.

A way of someone else solving your problems for you

Coaching is based on the principle that an individual is ultimately responsible for their lives and the results they're getting. If we acknowledge that we are responsible for something, it follows that we have power and influence over it. For example, if you're not getting the results at work that you want, a coach might encourage you to:

➡ Understand that situation more clearly.

➡ Develop new ideas or approaches for such situations.

➡ Take constructive action that gets you the results you want.

What a coach will not do is instruct you to go and do something specific, or go and do it for you. If they did, the coach would be taking responsibility – and so power – away from you.

What you can expect from your coach

The role of coach provides a kind of support distinct from any other. Your coach will focus solely on your situations with the kind of attention and commitment that you rarely experience elsewhere.

Your coach will listen to you, with a genuine curiosity to understand who you are, what you think and generally how you experience the world. Your coach will reflect back to you, with the kind of objective assessment that creates real clarity. During conversations, your coach will encourage you to rise to challenges, overcome obstacles and get into action.

A coaching relationship is like no other, simply because of its combination of objective detachment and commitment to the goals of the individual.

Because the relationship is based on trust and openness, the contents of your discussions will be confidential. Where a third party has requested the coaching for you, we will agree with you the best way to keep them involved or updated.

What your coach will expect from you

In return, your coach will encourage you to stay committed to the coaching process. That means showing up for sessions, taking your own notes where appropriate, and keeping any agreements you make during sessions.

In addition, your coach needs you to be open to the potential of coaching. That means contributing to conversations honestly and openly. For example, if something isn't working, your coach needs to know. If you have concerns or problems, voice them. If you know why a problem is occurring, say so. The strength and power of coaching relates strongly to the level of openness and trust between the coach and the coachee.

How might coaching benefit you?

The following questions will help you begin to form goals for a coaching relationship. They are not intended to identify specifics, but rather encourage thoughts or ideas.

Please take a few minutes to sit quietly with the questions, writing down your answers on a blank sheet of paper.

1   **What current goals (if any) do you have relating to the following areas:**

(a) Your work, e.g.

➡ Personal performance/effectiveness

➡ Career development, progression

➡ Ability to lead/manage others

➡ Motivation, fulfilment.

(b) Your lifestyle, e.g.

➡ Work/Life balance

- ⇒ Social life

- ⇒ Hobbies/Interests.

(c) Your relationships with others, e.g.

- ⇒ Your partner

- ⇒ Your immediate family

- ⇒ Your friends

- ⇒ Your extended family, i.e. relatives.

(d) Your learning/development, e.g.

- ⇒ Life experiences

- ⇒ Formal training/development.

(e) Your sense of contribution, e.g.

- ⇒ At work

- ⇒ At home

- ⇒ In your community.

(f) Your health/well-being, e.g.

- ⇒ Health

- ⇒ Nutrition and eating patterns

- ⇒ Fitness, exercise, relaxation etc.

2 **Thinking about your current circumstances:**

- ⇒ What would you like to do less of?

- ⇒ What would you like to do more of?

3 **What would you most like to change right now if you could?**

4 **What's going really well for you right now and you'd like to build on? E.g. do more of it, or make it even better.**

5 **In what ways do you currently obtain learning?**

➡ By experience, i.e. doing things

➡ Formal study, e.g. taking qualifications

➡ Through observation of others

➡ Reading, listening to audiotapes, etc.

➡ Structured training, i.e. courses

➡ Mentoring or coaching relationships, e.g. discussion, feedback.

6 **How much does your level and style of learning support your goals and objectives?**

Appendix summary **Coaching overview**

Hopefully, you'll now have gained a better understanding of the opportunity of coaching. Perhaps you've also begun to think about your own situations and goals, and are beginning to imagine how coaching might support you.

If you are preparing for a coaching relationship, please bring your responses to the above questions to your coaching session. Your coach will then be able to help you clarify your thoughts and ideas further.

Index

Enjoyed this book?

We hope so. And we'd love to hear from you – what you thought of it
and your personal experiences of coaching – from either side of
the table.

You can email your comments direct to the author and/or to the
publishing team via **www.business-minds.com** (click on the feedback
button).

So, whether you'd like to share a real-life anecdote or experience of
your own, or whether you'd like to tell us what you think and what
you'd like to read more about, just drop us a line. We'd be delighted to
hear from you.

Prentice Hall Business

More power to your

[business-mind]

Even at the end there's more we can learn. More that *we* can learn from your experience of this book, and more ways to add to *your* learning experience.

For who to read, what to know and where to go in the world of business, visit us at **business-minds.com**.

Here you can find out more about the people and ideas that can make you and your business more innovative and productive. Each month our e-newsletter, *Business-minds Express*, delivers an infusion of thought leadership, guru interviews, new business practice and reviews of key business resources directly to you. Subscribe for free at

▶ **www.business-minds.com/goto/newsletters**

Here you can also connect with ways of putting these ideas to work. Spreading knowledge is a great way to improve performance and enhance business relationships. If you found this book useful, then so might your colleagues or customers. If you would like to explore corporate purchases or custom editions personalised with your brand or message, then just get in touch at

▶ **www.business-minds.com/corporatesales**

We're also keen to learn from your experience of our business books – so tell us what you think of this book and what's on *your* business mind with an online reader report at business-minds.com. Together with our authors, we'd like to hear more from you and explore new ways to help make these ideas work at

▶ **www.business-minds.com/goto/feedback**

[www.business-minds.com
www.financialminds.com]

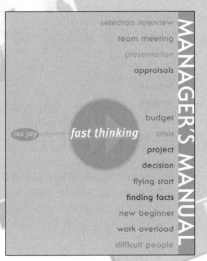

Fast Thinking
Managers Manual

Working at the speed of life

Ros Jay

0273 65298 2

It's a fast world with tight deadlines and you squeezed in between. What you need are fast solutions to help you think at the speed of life. This essential manual gives the clever tips and vital information you need to make the best of your last minute preparation. You'll look good. They'll never know.

The Fast Thinking Managers Manual – it is big and it is clever.

Topics covered:
Appraisal, Proposal, Presentation, Selection Interview, Budget, Team Meeting, Work Overload, Crisis, Finding Facts, Decision, Difficult People, Project, Discipline, and Flying Start, New Beginner

Available at all good bookshops and online at
www.business-minds.com

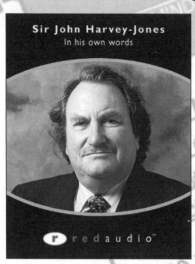